# THE LONG WAY HOME

# THE LONG WAY HOME

## RETURNING AMERICA TO HER FOUNDING CHRISTIAN PRINCIPLES

## JUDGE HAL MOROZ

NEW YORK    ATLANTA    WASHINGTON    TALLAHASSEE

# The Long Way Home

## Returning America to Her Founding Christian Principles

**Judge Hal Moroz**

Freedom is never more than one generation
away from extinction.
We didn't pass it to our children in the bloodstream.
It must be fought for, protected, and handed on for them to do
the same, or one day we will spend our sunset years telling
our children and our children's children what it was once like
in the United States where men were free.

~ President Ronald Reagan

*All to the Glory of God*

6

# The Long Way Home

## Contents

## Introduction

# The State of the Republic

Therefore hath the curse devoured the earth,
and they that dwell therein are desolate:
therefore the inhabitants of the earth are burned, and few men left.

~ Isaiah 24:6

America has entered a new era in its relatively short existence as a world power. Today we are led by forces that attack the very nature of our Constitution and our culture. A time when good is called "evil," and evil "good." And it is fair to say this state of being has developed over many decades.

The current state of our republic did not happen overnight, nor did most of our decline happen in secret. We watched as Leftist idealists entered academia and slowly chipped away at this city of a hill. They questioned the very existence of God, demanded tolerance for their deviant lifestyles, and entered our media and political institutions. They even entered our judiciary and began to make laws, in violation of the very charter given our judges and justices by our Founding Fathers. They removed the Pledge of Allegiance, prayer and the 10 Commandments from our public classrooms. They even had the audacity to declare that posting the latter (the 10 Commandments) "violated the Establishment Clause of the First Amendment" of the the Constitution.[1] In its 1980 *Stone v. Graham* 5-4 per curiam decision, the Supreme Court opined, "If the posted copies of the Ten Commandments are to have any effect at all, it will be to induce the schoolchildren to read, meditate upon, perhaps to venerate and obey, the Commandments."[2]

Just how on earth would posting a copy of the 10 Commandments in classrooms be a violation of the law? The First Amendment expressly states, "Congress shall make no law respecting an establishment of religion, or prohibiting the free exercise thereof." The First Amendment was NEVER meant to make our government hostile to religion. Doesn't common sense and logic suggest that barring the 10 Commandments somehow prohibits the free exercise of religion by school administrators, teachers and students? And what would be the harm in students and all members of our society understanding that it is fundamentally wrong to steal and murder or violate any of the other commandments of God?

And they have redefined marriage, the start of life, securing national borders, voting, citizenship, and our God-given freedoms and rights. They gradually and meticulously

---

[1] *Stone v. Graham*, 449 U.S. 39 (1980).
[2] Id.

undermined the very fiber of our national fabric. Today we risk losing the very Constitution and Founding Christian Principles that made America a beacon of hope in a lost and dying world.

Today, the mainstream media tells us we live in a so-called "Woke" society that preaches intolerance for opposing opinion, and destruction of our history. This "Cancel Culture" movement is a pernicious philosophy that demands racial reparations for man's inhumanity to man from centuries ago, but turns a blind eye to the inhumanity today directed against the most defenseless and innocent in our society. And here I speak of the aborted children, and those children that survived botched abortions only to be left to die alone on some metal table or in some closet garbage bin. A cruel act that the Liberal Democrat governor of Virginia had no problem with condoning.

And these are the same Left-wing voices that call for reparations from the descendants of slaveholders. And just to test the legitimacy of their outrage over "injustice," are they also demanding Japanese-Americans apologize for the treatment of American Prisoners of War at the hands of the Japanese during World War II? How about reparations for them? Or how about reparations for the descendants of soldiers during the Civil War who sacrificed life and limb so the slaves could be free and obtain citizenship and full rights under the same Constitution these "Woke" "Social Justice Warriors" now hold in contempt and seek to dismantle? Or are they hypocrites who have no problem with the inhumane treatment of human beings whose lives they do not value? I suspect you already know the answers. They are as reprehensible as the slaveholders of old, and have no business uttering the words "reparations" or "justice."

The long-feared "death panels" that would dictate the rationing over socialized healthcare finally came to fruition in New York and Michigan, amongst other Democrat-run states, at the onset of the COVID-19 pandemic unleashed by Communist China. Politicians like New York's governor had no problem ordering COVID-infected patients into nursing homes and senior citizen centers. Thousands upon thousands of our vulnerable senior citizens were sacrificed needlessly, especially when the Trump Administration went out of its way to secure safe separate facilities for those infected with the Chinese Virus.

We have entered a "Long Dark Winter," a subject I previously wrote about in my previous book, *The Long Dark Winter*. These were the words spoken by candidate Joe Biden in a different context, but nevertheless served as a harbinger of what would come if he had been declared the "Winner" .... and he was.

Joe Biden, who ascended to the presidency after a conspicuous absence from the campaign trail and questionable "vote" counting in multiple states, now declares, "No Amendment to the Constitution is absolute!" And he did so during a sparsely attended and viewed national address to a joint session of Congress on April 28, 2021. Biden's comments drew cheers and applause from the Democrats in attendance. An all-out assault on the very Constitution that codifies our existence as a freedom-loving republic endowed by our Creator with certain inalienable rights is well underway.

2020 was a turning point for America. We surrendered many of our God-given Freedoms and Constitutional Rights in the first months of the COVID-19 pandemic. Without a shot being fired, Americans accepted being ordered to "shelter in place," that is, submit to house arrest. And we were not under charge for any crime or diagnosed as being sick. That is a violation of the Constitution. We were ordered NOT to attend church. That was also a direct violation of the Constitution, as the First Amendment guarantees every citizen that the government "shall make no law" that "prohibits the free exercise" of our religion. Yet like sheep we followed the dictates of the government, that lacked the Constitutional authority to issue such edicts. And barely a word was spoken in opposition. Not in our pulpits and especially not by our Constitutional branches of government or the news media. As Biden now says with regularity, "No Amendment to the Constitution is absolute!" And now, we reap the whirlwind.

And Election 2020 revealed a pervasive, systemic voter fraud that has infected America and specifically targeted President Trump for defeat. That fraud, to any degree, is now declared "The Big Lie" of President Trump, his Administration, and the millions of voters who recognized the shenanigans that occurred in the Election of 2020.

When we turn our attention with a critical eye on the "news" we are fed every day by the mainstream media and the

Democrats, we quickly discover who exactly is telling "The Big Lie" — and it was NOT President Trump! The Left is monopolizing its razor-thin majority in Congress and the White House by spinning the truth to the point it no longer resembles reality. We were told for years that President Trump was "colluding with the Russians," but it was a lie. It was Biden, his son, and Democrat leaders in Congress colluding with America's enemies. We were repeatedly told "Trump supporters killed a Capitol Police Officer" on January 6, 2021, but this was NOT the truth. The only person killed at the Capitol on January 6th was a Trump supporter who was also a veteran of our military. This is not condoning what occurred at the Capitol on that day, it is correcting the record and telling the truth.

Unfortunately, our mainstream media has become nothing more than a propaganda arm of the Democrat Party. Joseph Goebbels of Nazi infamy would be envious.

Today we find Democrats in Congress and the Biden White House demonizing our law enforcement heroes and doing everything in their power to foist the divisive doctrine of "Critical Race Theory" to further undermine our Western Civilization. And the media is a more than willing participant in this narrative. They use the euphemisms of "reinventing policing" and "racial equity" to literally abolish policing and promote racism, respectively. We live in an era where good is called "evil," and evil "good." Violent felons have been turned into martyrs, and the Constitution itself, as I mentioned before, is under attack. And the purveyors of this insanity are rapidly moving to consolidate their power by using the

Pandemic unleashed by Communist China as a reason for passing legislation to curtail our God-given freedoms and rights guaranteed by the Constitution. This legislation is designed to cripple our economy, our election integrity, our culture, and our republic. It is a repudiation of the Biblical values America was founded on. The Left calls it being "Woke." It is anything buy. It is a recipe for disaster.

Today, on the heels of a year-plus state of hysteria brought on by a viral pandemic unleashed by Communist China and whose allies in our media and political establishments have fanned the flames of fear, we have surrendered our God-given Constitutional Rights and Freedoms and brought the America of our Founders to the brink of extinction.

But there is Hope ... and that is what *The Long Way Home* is all about! As dark as it was on that first Good Friday, the Easter morning that followed brought forth a new hope and confidence. And that sacrificial specter of the cross casts a shadow through time, even to the present day. Christianity will survive without America, but America will not survive without Christianity. Sodom and Gomorrah in Genesis 18 and 19 are stark reminders of the fate secured by communities that have gone astray.

So there is no doubt: America has gone astray! We are in danger of losing our republic.

At the conclusion of America's Constitutional Convention of 1787, as the delegates exited Independence Hall, an anxious crowd gathered, wondering what the Founders had envisioned for the fledgling United States of America. A prominent socialite of the day, a Mrs. Powel of Philadelphia, caught the attention of Benjamin Franklin and asked, "Well, Doctor, what have we got, a republic or a monarchy?" Without hesitation, Franklin answered, "A republic, if you can keep it."

This, my friends, is a book about keeping our republic and stemming the tide of evil across our land. And these outcomes can only be achieved by returning America to her Founding Christian Principles. That is the focus and the central purpose of this work.

If you believe the world is headed in the wrong direction, when its once shining city on a hill — America — under its new Democrat-control of Congress, the Presidency, and the Judiciary has openly declared war on Conservatives, Christians and Capitalists, then this book and its message are for YOU! America's founding Christian principles and ideals are under attack, and this assault upon America and our families was long in the making, but the speed of our decline is breathtaking.

We no longer have a constitutional system of checks and balances. Our modern Judiciary has strayed from the narrowly defined role given it by the Framers, and has set out on a new progressive course, piloted by activist judges and justices, to divine laws that are anathema to the Constitution. It is a usurpation of the charter established by our Founding Fathers, and an affront to the God-given rights enumerated in our Constitution.

And to make matters worse, the Democrat-controlled Congress led by Nancy Pelosi and Chuck Schumer have now aggressively embarked down a path to break longstanding rules, like the filibuster in the senate, and rush through arguably unconstitutional legislation. Their proposed legislation includes dismantling our border security and any election integrity we may currently have in Republican-led states, and consolidating power in the federal government to control all elections, abolishing any voter ID requirements and opening the door to fraudulent votes by illegal trespassers that Joe Biden has encouraged to invade America through our southern border for a plethora of "free" government benefits, provided of course, they elect the same welfare-state purveyors – Democrats by any other name – to maintain and further perpetuate their Socialist agenda.

Our Founders feared such treachery and created Constitutional protections to safeguard our republic, such as checks and balances in the form of three separate but equal branches of government. But even now those protections are under assault by our mainstream media and their tentacles in social media platforms.

One of the most ominous specters to emerge is the rush to "stack" our Supreme Court with Democrat partisans. To accomplish this, Joe Biden, whose done an about face on his previous long-held position to not increase the size of the High Court and make it a political branch, has now commissioned a group of Left-wing partisans and token "neutrals" to "explore" increasing the number of Supreme Court justices.

Not to be outdone, New York Liberal-Democrat member of Congress Jerry Nadler has spearheaded legislation to increase the number of Supreme Court justices by four. The move is obviously designed to offset the Conservative impact of the three justices appointed by President Trump and confirmed by the Senate.

These are blatant attempts to politicize the Supreme Court and remove our founding safeguard of checks and balances to ensure the Supreme Court would rule against any unlawful, unconstitutional acts by the President or the Congress. Making the Supreme Court a political arm of the Democrat Party to effectively rubberstamp the agenda of the far Left would spell the end of our constitutional republic. I trust there are enough Conservatives in Congress and elsewhere to challenge the enactment of such legislation in court as unconstitutional and, as such, a violation of the law. And I pray there are enough constitutional Conservatives on the High Court to deny such a destructive and unlawful power grab. The Supreme Court exists to preserve the Constitution and to prevent the other branches of government from undermining it. This is a final opportunity to stand in the gap for the America our Founders had the God-given vision to create. Let us pray and hope the Supreme Court rises to the occasion and stands in the gap for America.

And it deserves noting that the Democrats are in a panic to unleash their disastrous agenda because they realize their razor-thin majority is fragile. They understand the heartland of America will not tolerate the abolition of our Five Freedoms found in the First Amendment or the rights embodied in our

Second Amendment. They realize that despite the mainstream media's silence on their diabolical plans, it will not stop well-informed patriots from mobilizing and ousting them from control of Congress in the 2022 midterm elections. This is another reason they are seeking to destroy any semblance of election integrity amongst the majority of states. Voter ID and proof of citizenship are reasonable requirements to vote in American elections, but they are anathema to the Democrat philosophy of open borders and non-citizen voting "rights."

The COVID-19 Pandemic unleashed upon America and the world by Communist China is a case study in using a crisis to topple a constitutional republic. Fear of the unknown "Novel Virus" prompted even our President to call for a shutdown of the economy and the lockdown of a free people, which were critical mistakes. And that fear prompted even our most trusted evangelical leaders to support the closing of our churches to public assemblies of the faithful and those who sought the truth of the Gospel, which was another critical mistake. The latter was also a demonstrative breaking with the express teachings of Jesus Christ, who repeatedly cautioned His followers to "fear not."[3] And this admonishment is echoed throughout the Word of God literally hundreds of times.[4]

Isn't Faith most tested in times of crisis and fear? Isn't Courage recognizing adversity and proceeding in the face of that adversity? Did we as Americans fail that test in 2020?

---

[3] Luke 12:32; Luke 8:50; Luke 12:6-7; Mark 6:49-50; Matthew 10:29-31; John 14:1; et al.
[4] Isaiah 41:10; Joshua 1 :9; Philippians 4 :6-7; Psalm 118 :6; 1 John 4 :18; Psalm 23:4; 1 Peter 5:7; 2 Timothy 1:7; Proverbs 29:25; Psalm 27:1; Deuteronomy 31:6, 8; Psalm 34:4; Hebrews 13:6; Luke 2:10; et al.

And if we failed, is the damage done irreparable?

Faith was broken, and our God-given Constitutional rights and freedoms are being put to the test like never before. Perhaps the Rev. Franklin Graham said it best in a Christmas Eve 2020 social media message he posted for America. In it, he asked for prayers for both President Trump and our nation in the coming days, and Graham asked us to "pray that God would spare our nation from the evil that is before us." God-fearing Americans and Christians the world over are keenly aware this *Long Dark Winter* foretells a time of great evil by the forces of darkness.

But for Christians, this is a time of prayer and action. After all, we still celebrate the miracle of Christmas, a time when God Himself visited us in the flesh, as Luke 1:7 tells us, "To give light to them that sit in darkness and in the shadow of death, to guide our feet into the way of peace."

This is our Valley Forge moment. In that cold dark winter of 1777, history reminds us that General George Washington often prayed on his knees for God's guidance and intervention before confronting the evil forces of his time and ultimately gaining victory. Only time will tell how we react, and if our republic is ultimately lost. But I believe We the People still have a say in that destiny. Scripture tells us in 2 Chronicles 7:14, "If my people, which are called by my name, shall humble themselves, and pray, and seek my face, and turn from their wicked ways; then will I hear from heaven, and will forgive their sin, and will heal their land." The truth of the matter is we must act now because this *Long Dark Winter* is upon us.

And now the journey begins. The bottom line for our survival as a constitutional republic is prayer and work. We must take *The Long Way Home* and return America to her Founding Christian Principles!

~ Judge Hal Moroz

You and I have a rendezvous with destiny. We will preserve for our children this, the last best hope of man on earth, or we will sentence them to take the first step into a thousand years of darkness.

If we fail, at least let our children and our children's children say of us we justified our brief moment here. We did all that could be done.

~ President Ronald Reagan

# Chapter 1

# Founded as a Christian Nation

God presides over the destinies of nations.

~ Patrick Henry

It is the duty of all Nations to acknowledge the providence of Almighty God.

~ President George Washington,
First Presidential Proclamation, October 3, 1789

America was founded by people who believe[d] that God was their rock of safety. I recognize we must be cautious in claiming that God is on our side, but I think it's all right to keep asking if we're on His side. The time has come to turn to God and reassert our trust in Him for the healing of America...Our country is in need of and ready for a spiritual renewal.

~ President Ronald Reagan

We have been assured, sir, in the sacred writings, that "except the Lord build the house they labor in vain that build it." I firmly believe this; and I also believe that without His concurring aid we shall succeed in this political building no better than the builders of Babel; we shall be divided by our little partial, local interests, our projects will be confounded and we ourselves shall become a reproach and a byword down to future ages. And, what is worse, mankind may hereafter, from this unfortunate instance, despair of establishing government by human wisdom and leave it to chance, war, or conquest.

Only a virtuous people are capable of freedom. As nations become more corrupt and vicious, they have more need of masters.

~ Benjamin Franklin

America was founded as a Christian nation; of this I have no doubt. Despite what the historical revisionists and "Progressive" Cancel-Culture promoters may say, the recorded words and documents of our Founders are replete with references to Jesus Christ.

Examples of this historical fact abound. In a speech to the Delaware Indian Chiefs on May 12, 1779, George Washington declared, "You do well to wish to learn our arts and our ways of life and above all, the religion of Jesus Christ. These will make you a greater and happier people than you are. Congress will do everything they can to assist you in this wise intention."[5]

And John Adams, our second President and another Founding Father, proclaimed, "The general principles on which the fathers achieved independence were the general principles of Christianity."

President Thomas Jefferson, a Founding Father and our third President and author of the Declaration of Independence, exhorted, "I am a real Christian – that is to say, a disciple of the doctrines of Jesus Christ."

Patrick Henry, the first Governor of Virginia, definitively synopsized America's founding when he stated, "It cannot be emphasized too strongly or too often that this great nation was founded, not by religionists, but by Christians; not on religions, but on the Gospel of Jesus Christ. For this very reason peoples of other faiths have been afforded asylum, prosperity, and freedom of worship here."

Even the United States Supreme Court of yesteryear addressed the topic of America being a Christian nation when it held, in the case of *Holy Trinity Church v. U.S.*, 143 U.S. 457 (1892), "These and many other matters which might be noticed, add a volume of unofficial declarations to the mass of organic utterances that this is a Christian nation."

And President Ronald Reagan put the subject in

---

[5] *The Writings of George Washington*, Edited by John C. Fitzpatrick, U.S. Government Printing Office, 1935, Vol. XV, p. 55.

perspective when he addressed a prayer breakfast in Dallas, Texas, on August 23, 1984, and warned, "If we ever forget that we're one nation under God, then we will be a nation gone under."

I can only imagine what our Founders would think of the ridiculous, unfounded utterances of the Cancel-Culture "social justice warriors" who now declare we were never a Christian nation or, as Barack Obama once declared, "We are no longer a Christian nation." While the former is untrue, the latter is a topic of debate these days, especially when half of those who vote have no problem voting for politicians who openly advocate the killing of unborn babies. Support of abortion, Socialism, and a rejection of our Founding Christian Principles are a litmus test for acceptance as a modern-day "Progressive" Democrat.

Even in my home state of Georgia, we recently had a radical Socialist running for the United States Senate as a pro-abortion "reverend" [a supposed minister of the Gospel] and Democrat. I find this evidence of the truth of 2 Corinthians 11:14-15, "Satan himself is transformed into an angel of light. Therefore it is no great thing if his ministers also be transformed as the ministers of righteousness; whose end shall be according to their works." And he was elected! These purveyors of a different kind of "gospel" call evil "good" and good "evil," and substitute darkness for light.[6]

---

[6] Isaiah 5:20, "Woe unto them that call evil good, and good evil; that put darkness for light, and light for darkness; that put bitter for sweet, and sweet for bitter."

Perhaps the question of whether America can endure as a constitutional republic is best considered with regard to its moral underpinnings. We were founded as a Christian nation, with a reverence for God and His inalienable rights. But we have strayed. Perhaps not quite to the extent of Sodom and Gomorrah,[7] but we have lost our way. As Alexis de Tocqueville observed in 1835, "America is great because she is good. If America ceases to be good, America will cease to be great."

The Civil War, the assassination of several presidents, the scandals of yesteryear, even the war in Vietnam ~ all pale in comparison to the challenges we now face in preserving this "last best hope for man on earth," as President Ronald Reagan called her.

We are at a crossroads in America! One road leads to a continued republic, and the other to a Socialist dictatorship. The choice of which path we follow is still ours, but we are certainly running out of time to make that decision on our own. We stand at a precipice. America, for a variety of reasons I shall address, has been weakened at home and abroad. Perhaps a better word to describe America at present would be "crippled." Our system of checks and balances is broken. The power America once projected as a moral leader and proponent for good around the globe appears to have come to an end. The sun is setting on this shining city on a hill. The light we once projected has dimmed, and at risk of going out. These are the harbingers of the *Long Dark Winter* under the

---

[7] Genesis 18-19.

Biden administration and the Democrat-controlled Congress.

Joe Biden declared a second Trump Administration would usher in a "Long Dark Winter," but Democrats often accuse Republicans of the wrongdoing they themselves perpetrate, like Hillary Clinton and Stacy Abrams of Georgia refusing to acknowledge defeat were somehow forgotten when President Trump and millions of other Americans, including myself, question whether Biden ever came close to "winning" the legal vote in 2020. The overwhelming evidence of fraud that permeated the 2020 election is undeniable. We are in the midst of Biden's "Long Dark Winter," and it does not bode well for the America envisioned by our Founders.

I am a Conservative and I have historically voted for the most Conservative Republican in every election since 1976, when I cast my first vote for Ronald Reagan to defeat a sitting incumbent president, Gerald R. Ford, for the Republican nomination. But the voting irregularities and outright election fraud of 2020 should alarm every American, regardless of party affiliation.

President Reagan was my ideal of a statesman and American patriot. He embodied the Founding Principles I had come to embrace and articulate in my own life. His philosophy was simple: American government was based on our Founding document, the Constitution. This meant government had limited duties and powers, which were enunciated in that founding document, such as, providing for the common defense.

President Reagan understood that the primary responsibility of the government was to provide for the safety of its citizens. This is why we have a standing army, secured borders, local police and firefighters, courts, and the Constitution itself. Out of this controlling principle, the federal government had its responsibilities and the states had theirs. Whatever was not the dominion of the federal government as articulated in the Constitution was reserved to the states and We the People. This embodies the principle of federalism, which is codified in the 10th Amendment to the Constitution.

However, today, more than 40 years after I first voted, that philosophy of limited government and the notion that Americans could control their own destiny is lost. We now find the vast majority of Americans have lost faith with a system that they rightly feel has betrayed them.

In the past decade, America has gone through a radical transformation. This is no exaggeration. President Trump successfully reversed the rising time of regulations and taxes, a weakened and demoralized military, American embassies sacked and our Ambassador killed under the Obama-Biden administration [for the first time since the Carter Administration], the finest healthcare system in the world dismantled to fulfill the dream of a socialist in the White House [Obama] and his allies in the Congress, illegal immigrants running unchecked across our borders and corrupting our culture, America's standing in the world diminished, and the list goes on and on. President Trump is one of the few modern presidents who fought the good fight to return America to greatness.

At a time in our history when the great and noble deeds of our last generation freed a world from the tyranny of Godless Communism, we find a new emergence of that bankrupt philosophy in the very seat of our national government, with Joe Biden, Kamala Harris, Chuck Schumer and Nancy Pelosi now leading the charge to undo the positive strides of the Trump Administration. And there are many on the sidelines preparing to carry that corrupt banner, amongst whom we find the Democrat Party and their allies in the mainstream media.

Would my father, who died a month before the assassination of President Kennedy in 1963, even recognize the America of today if he were alive? Or for that matter, does the America of today even resemble the America that existed during the administration of President Reagan? Sadly, I think not to both. In many ways we are not better off than we were twelve, or thirty, or 100 years ago for that matter. But President Trump did improve America's standing in the last four years! Trump was better than his promises. He did more for the cause of Christ and America's working families than any president before him. He fought the prosecution of Christians for their faith at home and around the world. He lowered taxes and regulation of American businesses and our hardworking families. And despite the best efforts of Communist China, the Democrats in Congress and the mainstream media to obstruct him, President Trump engineered the greatest economic boom and the lowest level of unemployment in our history. He even brought back the popular refrain of "Merry Christmas" during one of the most treasured and sacred times of the year on the Christian calendar. And even after the pandemic was unleashed by Communist China, it was the Democrats in key economic centers that persisted with their fearmongering and business lockdowns that crippled our economic recovery and caused unemployment to surge.

The Democrats obstructed and fought President Trump at every turn, and they effectively tipped the scales in the electoral process to their dependents in this new age welfare state. And in many jurisdictions they have removed any requirement for voters to positively identify themselves as eligible to legally vote, effectively opening the door to election fraud with unverified mail-in ballots and giving ineligible persons (illegals, felons, dead people, non-residents, the underage, etc.) a perceived "right" to vote.

In the 1980s, despite the best efforts of President Reagan and those of us who proudly participated in the Reagan Revolution, Americans have turned their backs on the core principles which made us a great nation. We failed to institutionalize the Conservative changes of the Reagan Revolution, and their popularity waned. Led by Obama and his cohorts, the Liberal Establishment and their champions in the Judiciary and the mainstream media, quietly dismantled our foundational pillars. They held the Constitution and the Holy Bible in contempt, and effectively rewrote the noble history of the United States in our public classrooms and institutions of "Higher Education." As Obama declared, "We are no longer a Christian nation!" Joe Biden and Kamala Harris wholeheartedly subscribe to this philosophy.

Like President Reagan, who often declared, "America's best days are yet to come," I still believe there is hope. That is why I voted for Donald J. Trump to become President and supported his Movement to Make America Great Again. And it is why I voted again for President Trump in 2020. But I understand that this alone is not enough. Prayer and actively participating in the machinery of government to effect positive change is required. You and I must now follow through and actively support the agenda to truly Make America Great Again!

As long as we have Americans of faith standing in the gap for this "last best hope for man on earth," there is hope that we can overcome this prolonged transformation of America by the Left.

We might be approaching the biblical cities of Sodom and Gomorrah, but we are not there yet. Not by a long shot, not on our watch, and definitely not as long as we still have young Americans standing watch on the walls of this bright shining city on a hill.

It can be Morning Again in America! We have a brief opportunity to make America great again, but as I said before, that will take We the People turning from our wicked ways, and a commitment to a return to our foundational guiding documents and principles, those being the Holy Bible and the Constitution. And we must actively vote to ensure that all who would serve in the Executive, Legislative, and Judicial branches in our state and federal governments strictly support and defend the Constitution as written, as the Founders intended, and not substitute their will for the Law.  It will take such a revival, and it begins one person at a time, starting with you and me.

If my people, which are called by my name, shall humble themselves, and pray, and seek my face, and turn from their wicked ways; then will I hear from heaven, and will forgive their sin, and will heal their land.

~ 2 Chronicles 7:14

In a time when evil and darkness seems to prevail, Christ tells us once again, "Fear not!"

~ Pope John Paul II

# Chapter 2

# We the People

We the People of the United States, in Order to form a more perfect Union, establish Justice, insure domestic Tranquility, provide for the common defence, promote the general Welfare, and secure the Blessings of Liberty to ourselves and our Posterity, do ordain and establish this Constitution for the United States of America.

~ Preamble of the Constitution

You will never know how much it has cost my generation to preserve your freedom. I hope you will make a good use of it.

~ President John Adams

Now arrives the hour of action! Do not let anyone tell you it cannot be done! No challenge can match the heart and fight and spirit of America! We will not fail! Our country will thrive and prosper again!

~ President Donald J. Trump

If we have learned anything from the Chinese pandemic and its impact on America, it is this: Our Constitutionally guaranteed freedoms are fragile, and are only worth the paper parchment they are printed on, especially if we lack the will as a government and a people to maintain them. 2020 is proof of this statement.

In 2020, we collectively surrendered our Constitutional Rights of freedom of Religion (if the religions were fundamentally Christian, that is, Bible-believing Christians, or Judaism) freedom to assemble (in church, that is, unless we were out violently protesting the Trump Administration, and rioting and looting to further the Left-wing agenda), freedom of speech, freedom from arbitrary arrest, as governors and local state officials issued edicts subjecting average Americans to house arrest or "shelter in place" orders, without due process or charge of a crime, and a host of other unlawful, unconstitutional and downright un-American acts.

We surrendered without firing a shot and submitted like sheep to the dictates of government agents, who lacked the Constitutional authority to do as they did. We put on masks and stopped going to church under penalty of fines and jail. Pastors were fined and jailed, and still even others encouraged their congregations to comply out of fear and for "the common good." Yet even the Bible tells us hundreds of times to "fear not." And, as a general rule, not a word was spoken in opposition, not by our politicians, our judges, our clergy or We the People. Like lambs we had gone astray. So much for "Live Free or Die" in America.

Only a few voices cried out in the wilderness, and I was proud to be among them. I ranted and raved on every media outlet available that our country was losing its freedoms fought so hard for by our Founders and those legions of military members throughout our history, and we were hurdling toward a state of dictatorial Communism. I even entered the race the Justice on the Supreme Court of Georgia in March of 2020 to stem the tide eroding our God-given freedoms and Constitutional rights. More on that campaign at the onset of the pandemic later.

And the assault on the Constitution continues, with errant Democrat governors using the pandemic to spread fear and create dictatorial powers that are outside of their constitutional authority. They have ordered the repeated shutdown of small businesses, the suspension of family and extended family gatherings at Thanksgiving and Christmas to honor the blessings God has bestowed on this nation and its people. Even the celebration of the birth of Jesus Christ, once unashamedly heralded as a national holiday from sea to shining sea, and around the world by our service members, is on the brink of extinction. And make no mistake, this is not only an attack on our Constitution, it is an attack on Christianity, which has long been a target of the haters on the Left.

As I mentioned earlier in this work, at the conclusion of

America's Constitutional Convention of 1787, as the delegates exited Independence Hall, an anxious crowd gathered, wondering what the Founders had envisioned for the fledgling United States of America. A prominent socialite of the day, a Mrs. Powel of Philadelphia, caught the attention of Benjamin Franklin and asked, "Well, Doctor, what have we got, a republic or a monarchy?" Without hesitation, Franklin answered, "A republic, if you can keep it."

We are at tipping point in deciding whether or not to keep our republic. And make no mistake, we are at risk of losing our republic, and the God-given freedoms and rights codified in our Constitution.

As I recently shared with my friends Paul and Vickie of The Lighthouse WECC Christian radio station and Donna Fiducia and Don Neuen of Cowboy Logic Radio, my concern about this Long Dark Winter is that it will herald the end of our constitutional republic, and with it an end to Christian and Conservative radio across America and around the world. It is also why I chose for the cover of this book a picture of The Lighthouse under a foreboding winter sky. It is really a picture of America's freedoms and Founding Principles under siege. Ministries like the Lighthouse share the last best hope for mankind, that being, the Good News of Jesus Christ. The Lighthouse WECC Christian radio station in St. Marys, Georgia, is one such voice, a refuge of Freedom that stands as a beacon of Hope, shining the light of the Gospel unto all the world as Jesus commands in Mark 16:15, and it does so powerfully over radio airwaves and the worldwide internet. It is a critical, life-changing, nation-saving message. And as

President Reagan once said, "If we lose freedom here, there is no place for us to escape to … This is the last stand on earth." He was right. It is.

A *Long Dark Winter* is upon us. And I say this with a profound sense of sadness. All across our land, subversive forces in our society seek to undermine and destroy the very foundations of our country. And what are the foundations of America? Well, to paraphrase several American presidents since the Founding Father of our country, President George Washington, "The foundations of America are the Constitution and the Bible."

In California, proud liberal Governor Gavin Newsom outlawed Church services and even home Bible studies, and threatens criminal prosecutions with jailtime and fines of $1,000 a day for those who violate his dictates. This is un-Constitutional, because it violates the freedoms of religion and assembly found in the First Amendment. And its enforcement would also be unlawful, as it would violate other express Constitutional protections against arbitrary searches and arrests found in the Bill of Rights for all American citizens.

And kudos to the patriots in California challenging the dictatorial actions of their governor. But even there, the corrupt partisans of their government bureaucracy are scrutinizing signatures on the recall petitions to a greater degree than their votes for public office in any primary or general election. Their political allegiances and heavy handedness are obvious and an affront to every fair-minded American, but this is the result of a California under the thumb of "Progressive" Democrats. In truth, these partisans are progressing toward their idea of a Socialist utopia. It is an illusive pipedream that ends in ruin, much like Venezuela and Communist Cuba.

Make no mistake, this is also an attack upon the church and the Gospel of Jesus Christ. It is unconstitutional, unlawful and un-American. And these blatant attacks on Christians are eerily reminiscent of Nazi Germany's early treatment of Jews and others deemed "enemies of the state." And it deserves noting that California has no problem with its governor's acceptance and support of "peaceful protests," which is a Left-wing euphemism for violent mob assemblies that inevitably degenerate into rioting, looting and wanton destruction without consequences for the purveyors of such crimes.

In Oregon, you face criminal prosecution for peacefully gathering with more than six members of your family to celebrate Thanksgiving or Christmas, but "Peaceful Protests" in the form of rioting or looting are just fine. The rioting anarchists overwhelm our law enforcement community, then the Liberal media mouthpieces for these anarchists convince useful idiots in our county and city legislative bodies to defund our police. And in the recent election, this state decriminalized a wide array of dangerous drugs, including Cocaine and Meth. The cities of Sodom and Gomorrah would fit right in.

And if that wasn't enough, Oregon's Left-wing Democrat governor, Kate Brown, literally suggested to the press that people should call the police on any of their neighbors celebrating Thanksgiving with what they deem to be an "unacceptable" number of family members. The stated reason cited for such an unconstitutional overreach is "public safety." If unstopped, it is only a matter of time before the unvaccinated, and perhaps Christians and most definitely gun-owning American citizens are asked for their "papers" and denied their most fundamental freedoms to assemble and speak and shop for the essentials of life. Sound familiar from our study of history and its Socialist dictatorships? The Gestapo and admirers of Fidel Castro would be proud.

Adding to this perpetuation of fear and the thought that the government is omnipotent, we have politicians mandating the wearing of masks, even in our own homes. After all, they call the wearing masks a "sign of caring" for others and "proper public clothing." Joe Biden even calls the wearing of masks AFTER being vaccinated "patriotic." These are ironically the same things they once said about burkas in Islamic states, but of course they are not. They are a symbol of submission. If masks were as effective as the "experts" suggest, they would have material specifications, much like surgical masks or military gas masks, and they would be disposed of as biological waste and hazardous material, especially since they supposedly work to trap the dreaded COVID-19 virus, which has killed less people than the flu, cigarette smoking or the abortion industry, according to revised studies on the true impact of the Chinese virus; it is a killer, but evidence would suggest its impact calculations have been exaggerated. And the Left has approved the public shaming of those Americans who embrace their individual liberties and dare not conform to the mandates, in some cases even invoking criminal penalties, which I would argue are unconstitutional and unlawful.

Who would have believed this loss of our Constitutional freedoms anywhere in America just a generation ago? But as President Ronald Reagan declared in my youth:

"Freedom is never more than one generation
away from extinction.
We didn't pass it to our children in the bloodstream.
It must be fought for, protected, and handed on for them to do
the same, or one day we will spend our sunset years telling
our children and our children's children what it was once like
in the United States where men were free."

But there are some signs of hope! And thanks to the foresight of President Trump and the Republican senate of 2020, a Thanksgiving message was sent to America in a shot across the bow of those forces that seek to end the Constitutional freedoms that have so long been taken for granted.

In a 5-4 decision,[8] the United States Supreme Court took a stand against the unrelenting attack on America's first freedom, found in the First Amendment to the Constitution. This is the Freedom of Religion.

---

[8] *Roman Catholic Diocese of Brooklyn, New York v. Andrew M. Cuomo, Governor of New York*, 592 U.S. ___ (2020). On Application for Injunctive Relief. November 25, 2020.

New York's disgraced Democrat Governor Andrew Cuomo, who led the nation in COVID-19 deaths due to his bungling and mismanagement of the response to the Chinese pandemic, hand no problem with ordering the deaths of New York's elderly population by injecting scores of COVID-infected patients into senior citizen centers and nursing homes. But when it came to Constitutionally protected religious gatherings for Christians and Jews, Cuomo, like so many of his bigoted fellow-Democrats in California and elsewhere, ordered that religious gatherings would comply with his idea of what was acceptable in numbers and type of worship, or they would face criminal penalties and fines. Curious that the governor's wrath was directed only toward Christians and Jews.

The United States Supreme Court, led by Constitutionalists Thomas, Alito, and President Trump's nominees-turned-justices Gorsuch, Kavanaugh, and Barrett, rejected Cuomo's assault on the Constitution.

Justice Neil Gorsuch, concurring with the majority, wrote, "It is time – past time – to make plain that, while the pandemic poses many grave challenges, there is no world in which the Constitution tolerates color-coded executive edicts that reopen liquor stores and bike shops but shutters churches, synagogues."

Justice Amy Coney Barrett joined her four Conservative fellow-justices in blocking the unconstitutional edicts, whereas the justice she succeeded, Justice Ginsburg, anchored 5-4 majorities the other way.

This decision also marks the first of many promising long-range impacts of President Donald Trump's nominees on the Court and our country.

Chief Justice Roberts joined his Liberal colleagues on the bench in dissent of the opinion, making it clear he would continue to obstruct any defense of the Constitutional freedoms that conflicted with his personal agenda. This was not totally unexpected, as Roberts previously perverted the Constitution on numerous other occasions, including his joining with the Liberals to enact ObamaCare and continue the process of Socializing the republic and dismantling America's superior healthcare system.

In a victory for the Constitution and our republic, the opinion declared that "[E]ven in a pandemic, the Constitution cannot be put away and forgotten. The restrictions at issue here, by effectively barring many from attending religious services, strike at the very heart of the First Amendment's guarantee of Religious Liberty."

At a time of great challenges to our freedoms of speech, religion, assembly, and even fair elections, we should especially give thanks to God for the wisdom granted President Trump in fighting to establish a majority of Constitutional Conservatives on the United States Supreme Court worthy of our Constitution and the aspirations of our Founders.

To be worthy of our God-given Constitutional rights and freedoms, we must always be vigilant to protect and defend them for all Americans. This is where our individual voices are so critical!

This vigilance is also required on the system by which we elect our representatives in this republic. As we have witnessed in our most recent Presidential Election, there exists a persistent concerted effort to undermine the will of the American people by forces philosophically opposed to our Founding Principles, and they reside in Democrat strongholds that have perverted the proposition that We the People, the legal citizens of America, elect our representatives. And that fact was made clear in a December 2020 filing by the great State of Texas to the United States Supreme Court, which was joined by a multitude of other states, on how another group of political partisans disenfranchised the whole of America by polluting the electorate with illegal votes. That filing is easily found in a search of the internet, and it underscores the absolute necessity for a state and federal judiciary that adheres to the Supreme Law of the Land, that being the United States Constitution. That Constitution is a legacy of the Divine influence on our Founders and a codification of the God-given rights and freedoms we have enjoyed for more than two centuries. And now we put the continued existence of these rights and freedoms to the test.

Unfortunately, the Supreme Court even now continues to vacillate, as it dismissed the Texas lawsuit for what it called a "lack of standing." But those within earshot of the Court's deliberations behind closed doors report the decision to dismiss was led by Chief Justice Roberts, who reportedly feared "riots" if the Supreme Court intervened to correct the widespread vote fraud. And Roberts was joined in his moral cowardice by the Liberal justices and even President Trump's three nominees. It was a disappointing turn of events, especially when much of the country shared the President's hopes that the newly constituted Court would demonstrate wisdom and courage. It did not.

This book honors our country, the Law of God and man, and the legions of brave young Americans who fought and died to preserve our republic and defend its Constitution during this perilous time. The Supreme Court broke trust with the Constitution and the people of America, who appointed and confirmed each justice to the High Court through our elected representatives. And I present this work as a former soldier who served this country, and as a lawyer, educator, prosecutor, and a former judge. I speak as a citizen here, still possessing a constitutional right to the freedom of speech, and I do so for the purpose of promoting the kind of grassroots change that can restore the Supreme Court and our lower courts, and our constitutional system of checks and balances.

We surrendered many of our God-given Freedoms and Constitutional Rights in the first months of the COVID-19 pandemic. Without a shot being fired, Americans accepted being ordered to "shelter in place," that is, submit to house arrest. And we were not under charge for any crime or diagnosed as being sick. We were ordered NOT to attend church, because doing so would subject those seeking to practice their Christian faith to arrest. This was a direct violation of the Constitution, as the First Amendment guarantees every citizen that the government "shall make no law" that "prohibits the free exercise" of our religion. Yet like sheep we followed the dictates of the government, that lacked the Constitutional authority to issue such edicts. And barely a word was spoken in opposition, especially by our Judiciary. I spoke about this at length in an interview on The Lighthouse WECC radio, which can be found on YouTube at "Hal Moroz for Georgia Supreme Court – The Lighthouse WECC Interview" and on my website at MorozLaw.com. But this state of affairs was years in the making.

*Marbury v. Madison*[9] was the landmark Supreme Court case that established the doctrine of Judicial Review and set in stone the role of judges and justices in our Constitutional system of checks and balances. Judges and justices are there to interpret the law as written, not make up law. Their duty is to ensure the Constitution is upheld, not usurped.

However, on June 25, 2015, the Supreme Court broke trust with that precedent, the United States Constitution, and We the People of America! In *King v. Burwell*, the Supreme Court changed the express words of the legislation passed by the U.S. Congress, and substituted their will for the Law.

The very next day, in *Obergefell v. Hodges*, the Supreme Court again broke trust and usurped the Constitutional jurisdiction of the states and the people, and rewrote 5,000 years of an established definition of marriage and fabricated Constitutional protections for a deviant class it supported.

---

[9] *Marbury v. Madison*, 5 U.S. 137 (1803).

In the words of the late, great Justice Antonin Scalia in his *Obergefell* dissent, "This is a naked judicial claim to legislative —indeed, super-legislative—power; a claim fundamentally at odds with our system of government...A system of government that makes the People subordinate to a committee of nine unelected lawyers does not deserve to be called a democracy."

The primary purpose of this book, *The Long Way Home*, is to serve as a wakeup call about the critical nature of the ominous path we as a nation have embarked upon, righting the wrongs of the 2020 Election, and to declare the Constitutionally established role of our citizens – You and me – in keeping our republic. We have a duty to actually know who we elect as representatives and their policies. This includes those we elect to the Presidency and the Congress, and, at the state-level, our governors, legislators, judges, mayors and city council members, to name a few. Our votes for statesmen and women to these positions of public trust are vital to the survival of our republic.

Under our Constitution, the government exists to perform a well-defined function. It is NOT the master of We the People, and it was designed to be manned by public servants in our republican form of government. The Judiciary, for example, does not exist to make laws and impose its will on We the People. But, unfortunately, our modern Judiciary has strayed from that narrowly defined role, and has set out on a new progressive course, piloted by activist judges and justices, to divine laws that are anathema to the Constitution. It is a usurpation of the charter established by our Founding

Fathers, and an affront to the God-given rights enumerated in our Constitution. It is a Constitutional crisis.

I have a vision of what our Judiciary should be, based on my understanding of the Constitution and our Founding Christian Principles as a nation. And having a vision is important. In Proverbs 29:18, we read, "Where there is no vision, the people perish: but he that keepeth the law, happy is he."

When William F. Buckley, Jr., ran for mayor of the city of my youth, he ran against a liberal, John V. Lindsay, and lost. That was in 1965, and a year later, Buckley wrote a book, *The Unmaking of a Mayor*. He lost the battle, but ultimately won the war. Through his outspoken, sometimes unpopular, championship of Conservative principles, Buckley breathed life into ideas as old as the republic, in a society that was overwhelmed by a liberal, politically correct philosophy. His was a voice on a vision that cried out in the wilderness, and millions of Americans, including yours truly, heard the call. Bill Buckley set the stage for the election of his younger brother, and one of my political heroes, James L. Buckley, to become the Conservative U.S. Senator from the State of New York following his election in 1970. And, more importantly, Buckley created a movement from a vision that culminated in the elections of Ronald Reagan in 1980 and Donald Trump in 2016. And it is why I ran for Justice on the Supreme Court of Georgia in 2020.

I believe each of us in our own way has a role to play in the betterment of our society. We have good works to do. As I often told members of juries in felony cases I prosecuted for the State of Georgia as an Assistant District Attorney, "The only thing necessary for the triumph of evil is for good men to do nothing." It was a quote from Edmund Burke, an eighteenth-century philosopher who criticized British treatment of the American colonies and championed the virtues of good manners in society and the importance of the Christian church as a moral stabilizing influence in the state. Burke is considered the founder of the modern Conservative movement.

I was a judge in the great State of Georgia. And being a judge is a great honor and a distinct privilege, whether on the state or federal level. It is also a unique experience, which entails great responsibility. It is quite different from the role of an advocate, although the two serve as officers of the court. A judge, unlike a lawyer, cannot be an advocate for either party in the courtroom. Decisions are made based on the facts and the law. The judge or the justice is the gatekeeper, the articulator of the Law, and a sworn defender of the Constitution, as written.

However, with the precedent set by the Roberts Supreme Court in *Obergefell v. Hodges* and *King v. Burwell*, judges are no longer confined to that ideal, and instead have been given license to rewrite the laws of the legislature and substitute their will for the law. The Roberts Supreme Court, I predict, will go down in history with the same negative connotations applied to the Supreme Court of the *Scott v. Sandford* decision more than a century and a half ago, but for difference reasons.

In reality, the *Dred Scott*[10] decision upheld the express words of the Constitution and the letter of the Law, but was vilified in the North for being out of step with the abolitionist movement. The decision actually addressed the legal standing of a petitioner to file suit based on the facts and the law. It highlighted the need for legislative action.

Despite it fueling the North's vilification of the Taney[11] Court at the time, the decision kept faith with the Constitution and the duty of the Supreme Court in the constitutional framework of our republic. That role is found in the Constitution and was established by the Supreme Court in its landmark 1803 *Marbury v. Madison* opinion. As Hamilton proclaimed in *The Federalist No. 78*, "The courts must declare the sense of the law; and if they should be disposed to exercise WILL instead of JUDGMENT, the consequence would be the substitution of their pleasure to that of the legislative body."

But even with this clear admonishment from a Founding Father, the Supreme Court has dramatically strayed from its Founding Principles, and there rages a great debate in the modern judiciary. Judges are divided on the limits of their power and their roles on the bench. Many of the Liberal persuasion believe their job is to interpret the law in an innovative fashion, even creating laws at times, to dispense a brand of justice that suits popular opinion or their own good pleasure. It is the type of jurisprudence that was exercised by

---

[10] *Dred Scott v. Sandford*, 60 U.S. 393 (1857), was a landmark opinion by the U.S. Supreme Court that held that immigrants who entered America as slaves and their descendants were not U.S citizens under the Constitution, and therefore had no standing in federal court to file lawsuits.
[11] Chief Justice Roger B. Taney.

the United States Supreme Court in 2015, and by the Florida Supreme Court in 2000 in *Gore v. Bush*.

I believe the United States Supreme Court erred in dismissing the complaint filed by the great State of Texas, and joined by 18 other sovereign states, in December of 2020. The dismissal was purportedly because the plaintiff lacked standing. But who can say the citizens of one state are not affected and harmed by the fraud of individuals in other states, especially when it comes to the consequences of a presidential election determined by tens, perhaps hundreds, of thousands of fraudulent votes? Texas had standing, in my opinion, but the United States Supreme Court – truly the Court of last resort – chose not to hear the case and the overwhelming body of evidence on its merits. As President Trump declared in a Tweet to the nation on December 26, 2020, "The U.S. Supreme Court has been totally incompetent and weak on the massive Election Fraud that took place in the 2020 Presidential Election."

The Executive Branch of our federal government also has a history of undermining the Constitution. Barack Hussein Obama did manage to keep one of his most ominous campaign promises of 2008: he fundamentally transformed America! Who would have believed that less than two decades after the 9/11 attacks on America that Obama and Biden would welcome tens of thousands Muslim so-called "refugees" into this shining city on a hill. We have since even elected them to the U.S. Congress. These "refugees," predominantly military-age men and very few women, have surged through Europe and America, achieving significant political influence in London and the state of Minnesota. And these hordes have already left a path of destruction in their wake. The state of affairs is reminiscent of that which beset Rome some 1500 years ago.

Even more alarming, as I write these words, millions of illegal immigrants have crossed our southern border and roam the streets of America in violation of federal and state law, and they now have the blessing of Joe Biden, the mainstream media and activist judges to remain in this land and take advantage of our legal safeguards and safety nets which were originally designed for legal citizens. These include privileges of free healthcare, welfare, immunity granted by sanctuary cities, and freedom to vote in any election without the benefit of having to prove who they are. While identification cards are required to receive access to the most basic resources in our society, illegal aliens, with the blessing of our courts, need not identify themselves through the production of an identification card in order to vote. California and New York even issue them Drivers Licenses and the privilege to vote. The consequences of these foolish acts are destructive to our culture and national identity. This invites the creation of an electorate and a system of government that is controlled by a plurality of noncitizens motivated to vote by their benefactors who prey on their desire to receive free benefits in return for keeping their enablers in office via the vote. It is a state of affairs our Founding Fathers warned us about in the early days of our republic. It is self-destructive!

To combat the inevitable demise of the republic by these edicts, a vocal and growing movement has emerged. This is the Movement that was championed by President Trump, which has only increased.

This can be seen clearly in the 2016 presidential race, and in the election of 2020, where President Trump garnered 12 million more votes than he did four years prior. In fact, he received more votes than any sitting president in history, and his coattails prevented the loss of any Republican house seats in the Congress. Americans rejected the established politicians who reside in all three branches of government, and here I most certainly include the judiciary.

Trends in our modern Judiciary are alarming. I oppose Judicial Activism, where judges substitute their will for the law. I consider it a threat to the Constitution and our republic. And it is most certainly a breach of the oaths to the Constitution and the Judicial Cannons that judges and justices must abide by. I hold to the Conservative proposition that all American courts adhere to the strict interpretation of the Constitution as written and be consistent with the original intent of our Founding Fathers. It is emphatically the province and duty of the judiciary to say what the law is, not what it should be. If judges and justices want to make laws, let them run for legislative office. The judiciary is there to interpret the law, nothing more and nothing less. And that in itself is a great task. And this is one of the reasons for this work: To explain the substance and role of an elected member of the government, and the Judiciary, so We the People of the United States can make an informed and wise decision about the executive officers we elect to appoint judges and justices, as well as the judges and justices we directly elect. These are critical decisions affecting the future of our children and the continuing existence of the republic. This is our role in combating evil in our time!

Judges and justices hold positions of great trust and power. The latter must be exercised wisely, using great restraint, and with exceeding sound judgment. To wield that sword to satisfy his or her personal whims or desires, I believe, is a breach of duty and the public trust placed in that individual, and an act which is in diametrical opposition to the intent of our Founding Fathers when they established the Judiciary under our Constitution.

Justice Benjamin Cardozo said it best in 1921, when he addressed the debate in its formative stages during his time:

> The Judge, even when he is free, is still not wholly free. He is not to innovate at pleasure. He is not a knight-errant, roaming at will in pursuit of his own ideal of beauty or of goodness. He is to draw his inspiration from consecrated principles. He is not to yield to spasmodic sentiment, to vague and unregulated benevolence. He is to exercise a discretion informed by tradition, methodized by analogy, disciplined by system, and subordinated to "the primordial necessity of order in the social life." Wide enough in all conscience is the field of discretion that remains.

The year 2015 marked a definite turning point for the judiciary in America. The Supreme Court of the United States violated the Constitution in two back-to-back decisions. In its June *King v. Burwell* decision, six of the nine justices on the Supreme Court substituted their will for the will of the Congress and enabled the implementation of ObamaCare to proceed. These justices became lawmakers by substituting the words of the Congress for their own words in violation of their duty to the Constitution and the people of the United States of America. They violated a sacred trust!

As I recently mentioned to friends who serve as judges, the Supreme Court has made it impossible for me to teach civil procedure in good conscience. The activist justices have turned the process for deciding cases on its head. They no longer rely on precedent or subscribe to the principles espoused in *Marbury* and codified in the Constitution. They have become a law unto themselves.

In *Obergefell v. Hodges*, the Supreme Court rewrote more than 5000 years of established marital relations, and gave a new definition to marriage. They did this by manufacturing a connection between the homosexual lifestyle and the protections afforded American citizens under the Constitution. A razor-thin majority (five out of the nine justices) on the Court substituted their will for the Law and usurped the Constitution, in a manner much like they justified the barbaric murder of millions of unborn American citizens through abortion. In *Roe v. Wade*,[12] the Court expanded the notion of "privacy" to such an extent as to allow mothers to be exploited by abortionists and baby parts sellers to actually kill their babies. And the Court did this without regard to the constitutional protections of the babies under the Fifth Amendment to the Constitution, which states, "No person shall be…deprived of life, liberty, or property, without due process of law."

I believe Life begins at conception, and science supports that proposition, especially since the days of *Roe v. Wade*. Nevertheless, the topic of Abortion is political, but the issue of Life and the Law in America is fixed by our Constitution. Life is protected under the Constitution. Life is an enumerated God-given right under our Constitution, which cannot be extinguished without Due Process. Abortion on demand is unconstitutional and a violation of the rights of our most vulnerable citizens, our unborn living children. I find it fascinating that our scientific community searches for "life" on other planets through the exploration of microscopic organisms, but shies away from the notion that an 8-month-old fetus in his or her mother's womb, with a heartbeat and emotions and dreams and all the features of a gendered human being, could possibly be a life. To call such a baby anything other than a human life, a citizen deserving of protection under the Law, is unreasonable. It is wrong.

These millions of aborted babies since the High Court's decision in *Roe* were most certainly deprived of life and

---

[12] *Roe v. Wade*, 410 U.S. 113 (1973).

liberty. It is a national disgrace and a level of barbarism rivalling Nazi Germany, Communist powers like China and the old Soviet Union, and Islam.  It is my hope in the years to come that America will investigate these butchers who kill these babies and profit from the sale of their body parts. There is no statute of limitations on murder, and if murder and other violations of law were committed, they should and must be prosecuted. The excuse of "I was only following orders" or "It was acceptable under [Nazi] law to do so" will not be an adequate excuse or legal defense. Our Constitution speaks otherwise.

Literally minutes after the *Obergefell* decision, I was on  The Lighthouse WECC Christian Radio (TheLighthouseFM.org) with its president, Paul Hafer, sharing my views on the unprecedented move by the Supreme Court to redefine marriage, which is specifically in the jurisdiction of the states, and aid Obama in his radical transformation of America and Western Civilization.  The Constitution was being dismantled before our very eyes. The High Court was aiding the Executive Branch in usurping the Constitution, and the Republican-led Congress was disavowing its sworn duty and its multiple campaign promises to the American people to stop it.

For the first time in my life, as I drove home from the court on that fateful Friday in June 2015, I seriously wondered, what good is a Supreme Court that forsakes its duty under the Constitution to support the tyrannical agenda of a chief executive, in this case, Barack Hussein Obama?

The unprecedented rise of outsiders to the political process like Donald Trump in 2016 and others like Marjorie Taylor Greene to Congress in northwest Georgia in 2020 is evidence of the broad-based rejection by the American people of politics as usual. And fueling this rejection is the conduct of so-called "opposition-party" leaders in the GOP. These men were given a mandate and control of the American Congress to oppose the fundamentally flawed transformational agenda of Barack Hussein Obama. They utterly failed, and in many instances, enabled that destructive agenda to succeed. It was a betrayal of the sacred trust bestowed upon these men and women by the American people.

On issue after issue, be it ObamaCare or the treaty with Iran masquerading as an executive deal by Obama, the Republican leadership in Congress and the Judiciary failed the American people and the system of checks and balances guaranteed in the Constitution and the ruling in *Marbury*.

A consequence of Barack Hussein Obama's fundamental transformation of America included a death blow to the great American Spirit. This can be seen in a mindset that doubts America's exceptionalism. This is manifest in a multitude of naysayers who believe the construction of a great wall along the border with Mexico, the deportation of millions of illegal criminals, and the repeal and replacement of ObamaCare with an affordable and exceptional healthcare system is "impossible." And this is said in a country that has been endowed by God with the ability to do the impossible. We survived and prospered after a horrific civil war that pit brother against brother, went on to win two world wars, cured many of the so-called incurable diseases, and landed men on the moon and returned them safely to the earth.

With all the exceptional things America has accomplished, like building the Panama Canal through the Western Hemisphere, providing emergency relief and medicine to the world, and being a beacon of hope, just to name a few, I am stunned by the doubters. We actually have citizens, and men and women aspiring to the highest offices in the land, saying America can no longer do great things! How very sad.

And based on all empirical evidence, Joe Biden and Kamala Harris will only reinstitute and continue the destructive policies of Obama.

If this book has any message, it is this: America's Constitutional system is broken, but it is not beyond repair. In fact, it can be made stronger and greater than ever before, but it will take the concerted efforts of individual citizens to restore the building blocks of our republic. And vital building blocks of our republic are the Presidency, the Congress, the Judiciary, and the men and women we choose to stand watch on her walls. President Trump was the man for this moment in history, and so was Washington at Valley Forge, but now We the People must take up the banner.

Unfortunately, past presidents and the United States Supreme Court broke trust with the American people and violated their duty under the Constitution. The states have this problem as well. Many of our governors, mayors, and courts, by definition, have become lawless. But we can change this lawlessness, and it begins with a respect for the Constitution and the rule of law, and by understanding the role of those who would serve as elected officials, including judges and justices.

The Supreme Court and the Congress have unique Constitutional roles in placing a President's great power in check, and they effectively did so before the advent of activist judges and establishment politicians. These politicians found it personally advantageous to go along with or oppose whatever the chief executive proposes, ignoring the intent and constraints of our Constitution.

It is important to note a few things about Congress, despite what its current leadership may say. Congress exists as a co-equal branch of government with the Executive and the Judicial. It is responsible for making the laws. It is as important as the Executive and Judicial Branches in the scheme of the Constitution. And although more than 11,000 people, most of who were men, have served in both the House and Senate of the Congress since the signing of the Constitution, each member has a critical role to play in our republic. Consequently, the American public has a vital duty to fulfill when it votes for any candidate to hold an office of such high public trust.

President Donald J. Trump made the appointments of a new generation of judges and justices to the federal Judiciary, with three of them serving on the United States Supreme Court, and the Republican-led United States Senate confirmed them. But these positive strides have come to a screeching halt under the Biden-Harris administration. Nevertheless, we can change the Congress in 2022. It is imperative we replace the liberal activist justices, like Beyer, Sotomayor and Kagan, with strict constitutionalists in the mold of Scalia, Thomas and Alito. I find Chief Justice Roberts an opportunist who straddles the fence that divides the judiciary, often venturing into activism, as he did in the ObamaCare decision and *King v. Burwell*. The Roberts Court is a hotbed of judicial activists, and their alliance with the radical Left must be thwarted. This is a time of choosing!

As the Democrat Party has failed to differentiate itself from the far-Left Socialist wing of the political spectrum, and having ostracized its Conservative remnants years ago, electing Conservative Republicans is the only logical means to preserving this Constitutional republic and restoring our Judiciary.

I pray we choose wisely, to preserve what Presidents Lincoln and Reagan called "this last best hope for man on earth." Our duty requires no more, and our posterity deserves no less than the America we inherited. This is keeping faith with the Constitution, and a very American thing to do!

Freedom is never more than one generation away from extinction. We didn't pass it to our children in the bloodstream. It must be fought for, protected, and handed on for them to do the same, or one day we will spend our sunset years telling our children and our children's children what it was once like in the United States where men were free.

~ President Ronald Reagan

# Chapter 3

# Let Us Raise a Standard

Let us raise a standard to which the wise and honest can repair; the rest is in the hands of God.

~ President George Washington,
from his Address to the Constitutional Convention, 1787

Woe unto them that call evil good, and good evil; that put darkness for light, and light for darkness; that put bitter for sweet, and sweet for bitter!

~ Isaiah 5:20

We live in a time of cultural war. The societal norms we have enjoyed for centuries are being eroded before our very eyes. The vocal and often violent "Progressive" elements in our society have unleashed what is affectionally called "Cancel Culture." This small and predominantly Democrat movement has managed to pressure and threaten once reasonable segments of society to abandon meaningful and important historical truths and traditions. One example of their mantra is that there are more than two genders. There are not. Another example is that truly peaceful political assemblies in support of President Trump were super-spreaders of the Chinese virus, while violent protests in support of criminals and defunding our police were somehow safe and "peaceful." This is not true, nor is it scientific or reasonable, yet these malcontents champion such fictions with a hypocrisy that knows no limits. And, unfortunately, this slide toward the absurdity will only accelerate as we enter this long dark winter. The Democrats and their propagandists in the media will see to that.

It is hard to argue that the protective hand of God has not been on America. From our very birth as a nation, we have done what no other people ever did in the history of man. We were the first to gain independence from the Crown on the simple proposition that men are "endowed by their Creator with certain unalienable Rights, that among these are Life, Liberty and the pursuit of Happiness—That to secure these rights, governments are instituted among men, deriving their just power from the consent of the governed."[13] It was indeed revolutionary, and we succeeded!

We have since led the world in justice, technology,

---

[13] The Declaration of Independence.

scientific discovery, humanitarian outreach, tolerance of religion—you name the noble cause, and America has been there! One of the undeniable truths in this country is the faith of our Founding Fathers. They were men of God, who acted upon their beliefs. The fact we are a nation built upon a Christian heritage is undeniable! This fact is evident in the Declaration of Independence, the Constitution, and virtually every document of American historical substance. Seals on licenses, commissions and other official documents refer to "the year of our Lord." Even our money bears the motto, "In God We Trust." Our state and national legislatures and courts all refer to God at one time or another during session. Our Congress begins each day with an opening prayer. Examples abound!

Nevertheless, our culture, which includes our Christian heritage and traditions, is under severe attack in this long dark winter. We are bombarded by attacks from the Left to quash any reference to God or historical truths in our daily lives. Democrats seek to "Cancel" our culture! But for what purpose, and to what end?

Throughout our country, we have attacks on America's Founders and core values, statutory displays of our historical figures and the 10 Commandments and prayer in public places (not Islamic chanting, mind you), and classes that teach good citizenship. But the battlefront does not end there. Even reference to the 10 Commandments is under assault in our nation's courtrooms. Imagine that! Simple nativity scenes in our local communities during Christmas time are openly, and many times successfully, challenged in courtrooms across the land. And the list goes on and on. What is amazing, however, is not the fact people object to any reference of God. The amazing thing is that we have people in responsible positions willing to entertain and support such agendas, and, unfortunately, many of them are sitting legislators and judges. Think about it!

In just this past decade, the Supreme Court of the United States has taken it upon itself to redefine marriage to accommodate a vocal minority that sought not so much to achieve "equal rights under the law," as they stated, but to destroy an institution (Marriage) that was defined by God and embraced by civilizations for thousands of years.

During what has been called the "Greatest Generation," that is, the World War II generation of my father, the thought of American lawyers, judges and justices, Congressman and Senators rallying to the aid of terrorists being treated "inhumanely" in the Caribbean while American soldiers were fighting and dying abroad would have been unthinkable! But, alas, there was a new opportunity under President Trump. However, we have judges and justices ruling against an elected president [Donald Trump] they despised, and advocated for the so-called "constitutional rights" of foreigners, illegal trespassers, and those who invaded and continue to invade our country. Incredible! They give aid and comfort to the enemy.

Islam in its purest form proclaims itself incompatible with Western Civilization. Why are we disputing it? Better yet, why are our established political leaders in Washington denying it? And why are our judges and justices supporting this philosophy, which is anathema to our Constitution and our culture?

I realize such statements are controversial. Throughout my many years as both a student and a teacher, I have heard the old adage of never mix religion with politics. I have come to discover the complete lack of wisdom in that proposition. Politics is a struggle between ideas. What greater struggle exists in our day and age than that which can be found in the war of religious ideas? For Christians, that struggle is found in the spiritual realm. We follow the dictates of Holy Scripture, the foremost of which is the teaching of Jesus Christ. It is a religion of peace and good will.

Islam, on the other hand, is a political movement masquerading as a religion. It is a fanatical movement steeped in violence, intolerance, and the eradication of the infidel. Unfortunately for Christians, we are the infidels, along with our Jewish brethren. It is not a movement of coexistence. And it is an existential threat to the American way of life, the West, and all of Christendom. This is not my opinion, it is an historical fact. And we can ignore it at our own peril, or in the words of Shakespeare, we can take arms against this trouble and by opposing, end it! This was the central meaning of the Crusades. They were a great force for good that confronted evil in their time, defeated it, and ended what was known as the Dark Ages. The Crusades effectively opened up the Holy Lands for religious pilgrims of all faiths, whereas Islam sought to isolate these lands from the West.

We as a nation and as a people of Western Civilization would do well to remember the lessons of the Crusades. When evil is confronted, it is stopped. When good men do nothing in the face of evil, evil triumphs.

I appreciate the fact President Trump confronted evil in our time. He built a great wall along our southern border, and wanted to deport illegal criminals and the jihadist "refugees" Obama welcomed to America, end ObamaCare, stop the persecution of Christians, and recognize that the government is a servant of the people, and not their master. These ideas are anathema to Joe Biden and Kamala Harris, and the modern Democrat agenda they serve.

The Conservative "America First" agenda is still under fire by the Liberal mainstream media and others who should know better. And the more President Trump spoke of these issues, the more popular he became with ordinary Americans, as evidenced by the more than 12 million additional votes he garnered in the 2020 election. The more President Trump communicated directly with Americans, the greater the threat he posed to the establishment that favored Globalist policies and preferred the status quo. President Trump quickly became the target of their personal attacks. These attacks were formalized in illegal spying and lying to courts by operatives in the Obama-Biden administration, and the appointment of a Special Prosecutor with unconstitutional, unchecked "authority" and limitless jurisdiction to pursue Donald Trump in the hopes of discovering a crime in his past. This was anathema to the Constitutional notions of a presumption of innocence and due process. The idea here is: if you can kill the messenger, you kill the message. And their most recent act to topple the choice of We the People was to pollute America's presidential election through the use of easily corrupted mail-in ballots, easily hacked voting machines, and illegal votes, including those cast by non-residents of states that moved, illegals, felons, and dead people, just to name a few. This is not consistent with our laws or America's system of Justice. It is more consistent with Third World Socialist "Banana Republics."

In today's world, we have every right to be sceptical, especially when we look at the current Congressional leadership. These include Democrats who falsely accused President Trump of "colluding" with the Russians and even impeached him under false pretenses. And even the Republicans were given majorities to stop the creeping cancer of Socialism, and not only failed to stop it but wound up enabling it. Some questioned President Trump's sincerity as a populist Conservative. I did not, and I believe people can learn and grow and change their minds on certain issues. That's a part of life. But I do abhor politicians who make promises knowing full well they never meant to keep them. Joe Biden is a classic example of running on the promise of "uniting America." It was a lie. These are the leaders we see in the Democrat Party and in some cases the modern GOP. These members of the GOP are rightfully called "RINOs" (Republicans in Name Only). And I believed President Trump when he pledged to devote the full measure of his life to preserving this last best hope for man on earth.

And it is precisely because the political legislative leaders of our time stand on shifting foundations, that we must recognize the genius of our Founders in establishing a government anchored to our Founding Christian Principles, culture, and ideals, which are reflected in the Constitution. And if we are to endure as a Constitutional republic, we must do more than recognize our government, we must insist it stand firm on the solid foundations of America, which presidents since George Washington have proclaimed are the Constitution and the Holy Bible. If politicians violate the Constitution, they must be held accountable, at the ballot box and in a court of law.

It is time for a return to principled government with statesmen and women who serve as public servants, not tin horn dictators, and we need to elect legislators and judges who champion a return to traditional family values and common sense! The alternative is a further erosion of the foundations upon which this country was built. And that alternative is simply unacceptable! Why not base our fundamental core curriculum in grade schools back to the 3 Rs and the C, that is, Reading, [W]riting, [A]rithmatic, and [Good] Citizenship? And then reinforce those concepts throughout life? They served us well during the Greatest Generation and years before. Are we now too sophisticated, too technologically advanced a people to build a bridge of honor and integrity back to the fundamental values of our culture that made America a superpower and the moral example to the world in the 20th Century? I pray not!

America's college campuses are in chaos as well because of a numerical minority that aims to get their way, by force if necessary, and it has cascaded down through America's educational system. We are now raising a generation of idiots who know no better, because they were never taught properly in the first place. America must get back on track with extoling the virtues of a quality education, hard work, patriotism, Godliness, and selfless service!

Teaching for me has always been a source of enjoyment. The opportunity to directly affect the educational development of fellow Americans is an awesome responsibility, and it is one I have never taken lightly.

I began to formally teach college courses as an adjunct instructor with Central Texas College in 1984. At the time, I was an active duty Army officer, teaching on a part-time, evening basis. I taught American History and Government. Two subjects I have had a profound interest in since my youth. American History and Government—these two subjects have been much maligned in recent years. The latter for good cause, especially with the advent of the Clinton, Bush and Obama administrations of government-forced Common Core curriculum that has effectively re-written American history.

All too often, true American history, such as the significance of the Declaration of Independence and the Constitution, and with them men of character and integrity like Washington and Lee, and the impact they had on the shaping of the republic, have been erased from our children's history books and replaced with a politically correct philosophy that elevates men and women of questionable character and deeds. These are some of the Obama "achievements" I observed earlier. We have replaced truth with opinion, if not outright fiction. Combine that with the wholesale vilification of our Founding Fathers, the Ten Commandments, and the Constitution in this new-age Common Core curriculum, and we wonder what has gone wrong with America's youth?

Obama used his Bully Pulpit to lead the charge to incite violence and contempt for our members of the law enforcement community. Biden has taken up that banner in his own feeble way. Not mincing words here, even the mayor of Baltimore [and Secretary of the DNC] during the Obama-era encouraged and empowered rioters in the Spring of 2015; as she shared with the press, "we also gave those who wished to destroy space to do that as well."[14] What kind of examples have we set for our nation's children? And today violent felons are championed by the Left as martyrs.

Obama's legacy continues in the guise of the Biden administration with the lawless rioters, looters and anarchists of the "Antifa" and Marxist "BLM" movements.

---

[14] Baltimore, MD, April 24, 2015 - Baltimore Mayor Stephanie Rawlings-Blake held a press conference to comment on the riots in honor of Freddie Gray, a citizen of Baltimore with a long criminal history. When a reporter asked her how Baltimore police would respond, she said she instructed the police officers to allow rioters to express themselves and that "we also gave those who wished to destroy space to do that as well."

Thankfully, President Trump opposed that foolishness and lawlessness. His was and is a Movement that respects the Rule of Law and those who enforce it! But there is resistance to this.

My frustration with the state of affairs in the world of academia began in my college years in the latter part of the 70's. The radical student protestors of the Vietnam War era in the 60's seemed to take refuge in the colleges and universities across America. For many of them, their college deferments kept them out of the war, and permanently out of the real world. Many became tenured professors in those schools and went on to foment their philosophies in the classrooms. Many never hid the fact that they loathed capitalism, the military, the police, and any semblance of authority. They were the flower children of the 60's, and they took great pleasure in their new platforms to protest the American establishment, that is, traditional family values, hard work, traditions of honor, and faith in God and country.

I never accepted the liberal, politically correct philosophy they espoused, and I took exception in the form of debate. In high school, I was a member of the Debate Team and learned to look at both sides of an issue before I took a side and argued based on the merits. My outspokenness rooted in facts and reason often cost me in the form of grades. In the world of academics, at least in some circles, innuendo and emotion were the order of the day. All in all, I was better for the experience, and learned without a doubt that one must be willing to understand the cause they support, and take a stand when it is challenged. I have learned to respect many points of view that are not necessarily my own, as long as they can be argued with facts and reason.

My experience as a professor in Massachusetts was particularly eye opening. That period started in the fall of 1987. I was just assigned by the Army to serve a tour of duty as an R.O.T.C. instructor. Specifically, I served as an Assistance Professor of Military Science at the University of Massachusetts in Amherst. I also taught R.O.T.C. classes at Western New England College in Springfield, Massachusetts. We had many fine students, but they were few and far between. The overwhelming student populations had apparently bought into the Liberal mentality that presumed anything that had to do with the military was bad. The Liberals were intolerant and bigoted, which is what they called others who disagreed with their narrow points of view. They were the products of the overwhelmingly Liberal faculty members that "educated" them.

I recall many occasions during that two-year assignment, which seemed like an eternity, when several professors of higher education liberally displayed utter contempt for American values and traditions, and, of course, the military, especially the U.S. Army.

I vividly recall on one occasion writing then-Secretary of Education William Bennett to voice my concern about the state of affairs on that campus. The Secretary was prompt and gracious in his response, reminding me very much of the man who obviously had a great influence on his life, President Reagan.

What was the Secretary's response? Be patient. Stay focused on the important things. Be an example for others to emulate. Don't be discouraged. And continue to fight the good fight. Give 'em hell! Words to live by. And so they were. And I did!

Thanks to the intervention of friends in the form of Lt. Col. Michael Hodson, from my earlier days at Fort Benning, and Maj. Gen. Robert Wagner, whom I had met at Fort Bragg, my tour of duty in what we called "the Peoples' Republic of Massachusetts" was cut short to just two years, and I was off to an assignment as an instructor on the General's Staff at Fort Monroe, Virginia, on the magnificent Chesapeake Bay. My experience in Massachusetts made me appreciate a bumper sticker I once saw on a car along Interstate 95 on the Massachusetts-New Hampshire border. It read, "Live Free or Live in Massachusetts." That about sums it up. I have always had a soft spot in my heart for the State of New Hampshire and its citizens. What patriotic American couldn't help but love a state whose motto is "Live Free or Die"?

In later years, I would teach for a number of other institutions that took pride in the part they played in meeting America's higher education needs. I taught a wide variety of classes at the undergraduate and graduate levels, including Ethics in Business and Government, Decision Analysis, International Business, and Quantitative Methods. I found teaching as an adjunct Professor of Law at Florida Coastal School of Law in Jacksonville, Florida, particularly rewarding, both personally and professionally. Florida Coastal at the time was one of the newest ABA-accredited law schools in

America, possessing a diverse and distinguished faculty committed to an imperative of civility that fosters sound decision-making on the basis of informed and reasoned judgment. I respect that!

But alas, as we have recently seen in the State of Missouri, a university president was forced to resign over allegations and threats by a small but vocal minority over unsubstantiated complaints, aided and abetted by Liberal instructors and coaches. So much for the Constitutional notions of due process and the presumption of innocence. One instructor on the University of Missouri campus, an employee of the state no less, prohibited the freedom of the press and threatened mob violence against a student reporter. Not enough that this instructor was violating the Constitution or the rules of a civil society, this mob got their way. The inmates are running the asylums on many of America's college campuses. And they will reap what they sow.

In the interim, we should demand our representatives stop taxpayer funding of institutions like the University of Missouri and others that not only condone but enable the Marxist "Black Lives Matter" crowd to disrupt these campuses and our communities, and interfere with the students who actually attend classes and want to make something of their lives. Defund these so-called "schools" of taxpayer funding, and see how fast the Liberal instructors and community organizers wither on the vine.

Conservative Americans need to reassert themselves in these Liberal hotbeds that were once designed to train

America's future leaders. After all, it is the taxes taken from our hard-earned money that funds these places and provides the government-backed loans for these "students." No students who conduct themselves like the "students" we have seen on the Missouri campus should be receiving taxpayer funding in any way, shape or form!

Throughout my adult life, I have always thought it important to participate in higher education. To challenge minds to excel and think "outside the box," and build a better nation for it. To share knowledge with others and, in the process, become a more learned person myself. There is a value to sharing real world experiences and a philosophy born of reason. God knows the youth of America get enough of the other side. I like to think of it as a fair and balanced education.

Even in my campaign for Justice on the Supreme Court of Georgia, my campaign was met by intolerant voices that sought to prohibit my freedom of speech or even allow me to debate the issues of our time. And these intolerant voices included so-called "Social Justice Warrior" who were ignorant of the very rights that allowed them to spew their hate.

This was my unedited response to one such attack voiced to a local television anchor, Jim Wallace of WALB News, in Albany, Georgia, who had the decency to allow me to respond, for which I am grateful:

Dear Mr. Wallace,

Thank you for reaching out to me a short time ago to respond to allegations levelled at me. I appreciate you giving me this opportunity. My response is as follows:

When the words of any person over a lifetime are taken out of context, I realize they can be warped to fit any narrative. And I understand that politics is no place for the weak of heart or those sensitive to criticism.

I have taught United States history and the law, and have written about the same. They comprise dozens of books and countless articles over several decades. But some detractors of mine have taken words I have written in books and mixed them with fictitious social media postings to form what are anathema to my beliefs as an American and a Christian. And in that same context, I am informed that my detractors who take quotes out of context on historical figures I have written about, failed to mention any of my writings on people like Abraham Lincoln, Theodore Roosevelt, John F. Kennedy or those who penned the Constitution or served with distinction in our military.

So there is no doubt, I love the Constitution and the inalienable rights it espouses, such as the freedom of speech and the proposition of equal justice under the law, regardless of someone's race, gender, national origin or any of the immutable characteristics they may possess. In fact, I fought for those very rights as a soldier in the Army for the first 21 years of my adult life. And I have always aspired to conduct myself as a public figure in the highest traditions of the law and my upbringing. I am not perfect, but nor am I what others who do not know me would suggest I am.

But perhaps the most disheartening thing is that anyone would attempt to assassinate a candidate on the eve of an election for words in the public domain, not only taking them out of context, but actually mixing them with outright falsehoods about my service to our community and malicious fictitious tweets that I have previously disavowed as not being mine. But I realize this is politics, and some would choose to silence me because I chose to exercise my rights as an American citizen and support a presidential candidate in 2016 who some find abhorrent, but nevertheless serves as our president. And on that same token, I would never attempt to silence or discredit someone who held the opposite political beliefs, because, after all, this is America, where civil discussion and challenging points of view are a fundamental part of our lives and intellectual growth.

I am consoled by the fact that my reputation is best evidenced by the people I have encountered and work with and who know me for the person I am, not what someone who is a stranger to me and my values would tell others I am.

And to make it perfectly clear, as I have stated and will continue to state: politics and personal opinions have no business in a court of law or on the highest court in our state. My pledge is to decide matters based on the facts of each particular case and the applicable law. I will be respectful, fair and impartial. Nothing more and nothing less. That is what I have done and what I will continue to do, regardless of the outcome of this political and identifiably non-partisan race.

Thank you for the opportunity to respond.

At your service,

Hal Moroz

I often comment to friends that the young Liberal idiots we see today will eventually grow up, have responsibilities, pay taxes, and become Conservatives. But that seems less and less likely with the Democrat Party actively cultivating a base that is totally dependent on public welfare for their existence. Some call this the "Plantation," precisely because it makes its recipients dependent on their political masters, in this case the Democrat Party. This new poverty class in America will loyally support the candidate who promises the most government handouts. We have seen this in the popularity of Socialist Bernie Sanders, Hillary Clinton and now Joe Biden.

2 Thessalonians 3:10 states, "Now we command you, brethren, in the name of our Lord Jesus Christ, that ye

withdraw yourselves from every brother that walketh disorderly, and not after the tradition which he received of us." Such Holy Scripture was universally embraced by our Founding Fathers!

In the words of Thomas Jefferson, "The democracy will cease to exist when you take away from those who are willing to work and give to those who would not."

It is little wonder why Jefferson and the rest of our Founders are hated by the Left. Obama dedicated his presidency, and Hillary Clinton her political life, and Joe Biden his chances of victory, to eradicating the memory of these men and their Christian Founding Principles.

The perpetrators of this political correctness that once cried for "tolerance," especially when it came to demands that we accept homosexual lifestyles as "natural," now expect the rest of America to abandon their religious convictions and Constitutional rights. We see this in the violent riots and looting in Seattle and Portland, the ridiculous homosexual "wedding cake" stories, where many in that movement are not content with obtaining these extra-societal "rights," they now want the traditional values to yield to their perversions. They demand the expulsion of God and the Holy Bible from our nation's classrooms, and, among other things, the acceptance and federal funding of the abortionists and baby part sellers. Annual taxpayer funding of the abortion industry is approaching $1 billion. This is an unconstitutional "taking" against American taxpayers.

The level of depravity on the part of the Left is sometimes hard to fathom, especially with its prevalence. They advocate so-called "art" that depicts the Cross of Christ in a jar of urine, while at the same time demanding punishment for anyone who would exercise their freedom of speech by drawing a picture of, or criticizing, the so-called "Prophet" of Islam. And if the latter was done at any institution of higher learning, you can bet anyone exercising such a freedom would be summarily dismissed, and the entire school population would undergo hours of so-called "sensitivity" training, which is more like Liberal indoctrination.

Nevertheless, those same Liberal thought police demand the silencing of any reference to the one true God, prayer, law and order, and traditional family values. Where is their call for tolerance now? Their hypocrisy is crystal clear and undeniably evident. This premeditated attack on America from within is most alarming, and it brings home the meaning of the words uttered by a dear friend in years gone by, the late William E. Simon, our former Secretary of the Treasury during the Nixon and Ford Administrations, when he said:

> On the eve of World War I, Sir Edward Grey, the British foreign secretary, issued a somber and prophetic warning. "The Lamps are going out," he said, "all over Europe." That statement could be repeated now, with one important, chilling difference. The lamps are going out, not simply on one continent, but all over the world...They are even in danger of going out in

the United States—where the torch of liberty is supposed to burn its brightest.

I believe we were placed here at this moment in America's history to keep the torch of liberty burning bright, and to preserve and strengthen this last best hope for man on earth.

I believe that those of us who are able to share wisdom with our youth have a duty to do so. To neglect that duty exposes them to the pervasive and politically correct philosophy of the mainstream media, their teachers, and the Liberal politicians.

What ever happened to Education in America? And what about the idea that patriotism and civility are actually good for our society? We have removed morality and God from our nation's classrooms, and we wonder why our classrooms are in such utter shambles!

The question is: When does the insanity stop?

The answer is twofold: (1) When responsible parents return to being involved in the education of their children, instead of some socialist bureaucrats in Washington; and (2) when we elect statesmen who will stop appointing champions of moral relativism and political correctness to elected office and, particularly, the Judiciary.

This is another reason why I wholeheartedly supported the agenda of President Trump and our Secretary of Education, Betsy DeVos. Both set a bold vision for America's future that respects the foundation laid by our Founding Fathers. They understood the importance of the Constitution and an educational system that champions American cultural values. They saw an America that is exceptional and ready to be made great again!

The American people overwhelming reject the specious arguments of those who wish to expel God and prayers from our nation's schools and public forums. But for these judges who give life to these Liberal notions that are diametrically opposed to our traditional values and heritage, we would be far better off. In the name of political correctness we have effectively undermined, and continue to undermine, those foundations which made this country great.

Joe Biden and Kamala Harris' agenda is one focusing on the ultimate abolition of private property. It is a vision heralded by Karl Marx more than a century ago, and its modern-day champions are found in the violent inner cities of America's Democrat-run strongholds.

Yet, as these same violent activists decry Capitalism and justify looting as a form of "reparations," they would kill if anyone took their smartphones or name-branded designer shoes or clothing. It is a brand of Marxism that is best summed up as: Marxism for thee, but not for me! They are the failed ideologies found in the BLM and so-called Antifa movements. Ignorant, violent and identified by their double-standards. They are what Jesus Christ called "Hypocrites." And these Marxists know this, and it is one of the many reasons they literally hate Christianity. They are as barbaric as the Islamic State fanatics and their caliphate that President Trump and the United States military destroyed, something eight years of Obama-Biden never did, or perhaps more accurately, never wanted to do. They coddled and emboldened terrorists, from dropping off planeloads of cash to the Ayatollahs in Iran to "trading" one American traitor for five Islamic war lords to return to the killing fields of the Middle East.

The Obama-Biden administration was never about making America a shining city on a hill, it was about humbling America and bringing its citizen to their knees ... something the professional sports franchises and their ungrateful prima donnas do with ever increasing regularity. They are an affront to the legions of Americans who fought and died throughout our noble history to preserve and protect the God-given rights and freedoms woven into the very fabric of our nation and the Constitution.

And even as the Obama-Biden regime lingered in its lame duck existence following the 2016 election, Obama, Biden and a group of conspirators sought to use America's intelligence apparatus and legal system to thwart and overturn the Constitutional mandate of America's voters. They spied on the fledgling Trump transition team and presidency, heralding one of the greatest abuses of power in our nation's history. The consequences of which are yet to be realized. But this event horizon will define our continued existence as a nation of laws, as our Founders envisioned, or a tyranny that no longer values the proposition of equal justice under the law and individual liberty.

This abuse of power and the need to restore our judiciary and respect for the rule of law were major reasons I entered the race for Justice on the Supreme Court of Georgia in March of 2020.

And in that race, the good people of Georgia spoke, and incumbent Justice Sarah Warren won, and she won decisively! But when all was said and done, 446,026 informed Georgians cast their votes for our campaign to support the cause we embraced for good government, and a rebirth of respect for our God-given Freedoms and Constitutional Rights. And millions nationwide were alerted to the problems facing our society and our judiciary. So all in all, it was a good race!

What I did discover in my race was a yearning for truth and a return to America's founding values and principles. And I was joined by old and new friends in my quest. Old friends like former Judge Kathe Loeffler, Chief Shannon Brock of the Watkinsville [Georgia] Police Department, Paul and Vickie Hafer, Martin Turner, and Steve Curtis of WECC Christian radio in St. Marys, Georgia, and Donna Fiducia and Don Neuen of Cowboy Logic Radio, Audrey Russo of the REEL Talk radio show, and concerned citizens like Rindy Howell of St. Marys and statesman and former Deputy Assistant Secretary of the U.S. Army Van Hipp. And new friends like the Mayor of Valdosta [Georgia] and radio host, Scott James Matheson ... and the list goes on and on, more than 446,000 new friends and informed voters, who knew who and what they were voting for. No man or campaign is a failure with friends such as these!

My greatest concern was always the thought of disappointing those who supported me. I hope I did not let them down or make them lose hope in our future. President Reagan said it best, when he declared in my youth, "America's best days are yet to come!" He was right! They are! Believe it! I believe in the promise of Romans 8:28.

And so there is no doubt, I lost my June 2020 race for Justice on the Supreme Court of Georgia, and I lost a great many other battles in my life, and I have lost loved ones, but the Cause Goes On! And I have come to realize that failure is sometimes the first step toward success. "Lay me down and bleed awhile," Reagan said in 1976, when he lost his first bid to become President and unseat an incumbent. "Though I am wounded, I am not slain." As the Great Communicator said, "I shall rise and fight again." He did!

The truth is: America is in the midst of a very troubling time. As I have repeatedly said throughout this work, we no longer have a Constitutional system of checks and balances. Darkness has descended upon our country and has taken root in the Judiciary, starting in the United States Supreme Court and cascading down to our state courts, affecting even my beloved Georgia Supreme Court, where I have practiced the law with regularity. Our modern Judiciary has strayed from the narrowly defined role given it by the Framers, and has set out on a new progressive course, piloted by activist judges and justices, to divine laws that are anathema to the Constitution. It is a usurpation of the charter established by our Founding Fathers, and an affront to the God-given rights enumerated in our Constitution.

I say this as a concerned citizen who cares about the future of this republic, and I say this from a position of authority as a former judge and professor of law, as a prosecutor and as a bar member of the United States Supreme Court, who has practiced before the high Court, and many others.

We have descended into a nation with clearly defined battle lines, as stark and as clear as ever before, and I would include the Revolutionary and Civil War eras in this statement. The stakes were never higher, and the consequences never greater.

We have federal judges who actively opposed President Trump's plenary powers under the Constitution and substituted their notions on what the law should be. They barred the President from banning travel to America by foreign nationals coming from countries with a history of hostility toward the United States and its citizens, and this was done in spite of Congressional statutes,[15] Executive Orders, and the Constitution giving the President express authority to ban such threats. These activist federal judges have ruled that protections afforded U.S. citizens under the Constitution shall be extended to non-citizen foreigners in caravans outside of our country traveling north to our southern border with Mexico. They even perverted the 14th Amendment, which was designed to give citizenship to slaves, to somehow apply to illegal trespassers who give birth on American soil. Their rationale was that these so-called "anchor babies" are protected as citizens by the 14th

---

[15] 8 U.S. Code § 1182.

Amendment, totally ignoring that these are non-citizens, who are subject to the jurisdiction of their home countries. These are edicts by unelected judges that have no basis in law, but the Congress is unwilling to intervene and stop this perversion of the Constitution and, thereby, check the Judiciary. These non-citizens, like foreign diplomats, are the subjects of foreign powers, only these foreigners are here illegally. The 14th Amendment was never intended to give license to criminal acts.[16] We even have judges ordering the return of foreign criminals deported from the United States for their lawlessness back to the United States, in violation of state and federal laws prohibiting such actions. These are gross violations of the role established for our judges and justices in legal precedent and codified law. This is a Constitutional crisis.

If Joe Biden has his way, America will be a borderless sanctuary for illegals, and the recipient of unchecked Communist Chinese plagues the kind of which has recently ravaged the world. Thank God President Trump had the wisdom and the vision to build the wall on our southern border and ban travel from mainland China, both, by the way, over the strong vocal objection of Joe Biden, Nancy Pelosi, and Chuck Schumer, who accused the President of being a "fearmonger" and "xenophobe!" How wrong these Democrats

---

[16] The 14th Amendment to the U.S. Constitution was adopted on July 9, 1868: "All persons born or naturalized in the United States, and subject to the jurisdiction thereof, are citizens of the United States and of the state wherein they reside. No state shall make or enforce any law which shall abridge the privileges or immunities of citizens of the United States; nor shall any state deprive any person of life, liberty, or property, without due process of law; nor deny to any person within its jurisdiction the equal protection of the laws."

were, and how right President Trump was and continues to be in the wake of his tenure in the White House.

Since Donald Trump's initial nomination for President in 2016, the Democrats, led by Obama, Biden, and a cabal of conspirators in the Deep State bowels of our government, have gone out of their way to use every method, legal and otherwise, to derail the agenda of President Trump and blunt America's return to greatness. From illegally spying on then-President-elect Trump to concocting a false narrative to execute a coup under the guise of an impeachment, Democrats have irreparably harmed America … but all is not lost, and the cause goes on!

This book has hopefully provided answers to many of our problems, and contains the Founding Documents of our country, which include the Declaration of Independence, and the Supreme Law of the Land: The U.S. Constitution, so you can refer to the principles I cite. These are the blueprints for America's return to greatness, and form the bulk of ideas and principles upon which our nation was founded and must return to if we are to endure and prosper.

These documents are not great mysteries, as the media pundits and legal profession would have you believe. The Bible says its authors were holy men of old who spoke as God the Holy Spirit moved them.[17] I believe such can also be said of our Founders. Our Founding Documents extoll the principles upon which our nation was founded, and the role

---

[17] 2 Peter 1:21, KJV: "For the prophesy came not in old time by the will of man: but holy men of God spake as they were moved by the Holy Ghost."

of our state and federal governments. In the final analysis, these documents and this book embody a plan to reclaim America's Founding Christian Principles and greatness.

We have much to learn from our history, and the honor and traditions of the past, and those legions that came before us. History is replete with the downfall of nations who thought themselves infinitely wiser than their predecessors and Almighty God. The Tower of Babel and Sodom and Gomorrah immediately come to mind. God and country—I have dedicated my life to both, and have written and taught extensively about each.

During my own time as a youth, I recall a simple recitation we had in grade school following the morning prayer. It was written about America and set to music in 1831 by Samuel F. Smith. It has always served me well, and gave me pause to reflect on the past and my duty in the present. And it went exactly like this:

*My country 'tis of thee, Sweet land of liberty, Of thee I sing; Land where my fathers died, Land of the pilgrim's pride, From every mountain side, Let freedom ring… Our fathers' God to thee, Author of liberty, To thee we sing. Long may our land be bright, With freedom's holy light, Protect us by they might, Great God, our King.*

So, in this day and age, when good is called "evil" and evil "good," men who embrace our Founding Christian Principles and quest to make America great again are called xenophobic, or worse, let us stand in the gap for America and our culture. I am old enough to recall the same disparaging comments being hurled at Ronald Reagan in 1980 when he chose as an outsider to stand against the establishment and work to make America great again!

There is no better time to be alive in America! Men and women of courage are in great demand during this long dark winter. Let this brief shining moment count. Let it be said of us that we were not just marking time, but that we made a difference.

Americans are not a perfect people, but we are called to a perfect mission.

I thank God that my life has been spent in a land of liberty, and that he has given me a heart to love my country with the affection of a son.

~ President Andrew Jackson

Most people dwell in the Grey Twilight, which knows neither victory nor defeat. It is not the critic who counts, not the man who points out how the strong man stumbled or where the doer of deeds could have done better. The credit belongs to the man who is actually in the arena; whose face is marred by dust and sweat and blood; who strives valiantly; who errs and comes short again and again...who knows the great enthusiasm, the great devotions, and spends himself in a worthy cause; who at the least knows in the end the triumph of high achievement; and who, at the worst, if he fails, at least fails while doing greatly, so that his place shall never be with those cold and timid souls who know neither victory nor defeat.

~ President Theodore Roosevelt

# Chapter 4

# God and County

Beware lest any man spoil you through philosophy and vain deceit, after the tradition of men, after the rudiments of the world, and not after Christ.

~ Colossians 2:8

And be not conformed to this world: but be ye transformed by the renewing of your mind, that ye may prove what [is] that good, and acceptable, and perfect, will of God.

~ Romans 12:2

Love not the world, neither the things [that are] in the world. If any man love the world, the love of the Father is not in him. For all that [is] in the world, the lust of the flesh, and the lust of the eyes, and the pride of life, is not of the Father, but is of the world.

~ 1 John 2:15-16

Upon this rock I will build my church,
And the gates of hell shall not prevail against it.

~ Matthew 16:18

Christianity will survive without America, but America cannot survive without Christianity. As President Ronald Reagan declared in my youth, "If we ever forget that we're one nation under God, then we will be one nation gone under." He was right then, and that simple statement holds true today. Yet there are forces in our society moving us ever farther from America's Founding Christian Principles. We have examined these forces throughout this work.

And President George Washington, our Founding Father, warned us about entangling alliances with the world in his Farewell Address, and he warned us that "reason and experience both forbid us to expect that national morality can prevail in exclusion of religious principle."[18] And, as previously noted in Chapter 1, that "religious principle" is found in the Christian faith.

The Obama administration, and the Biden administration that succeeds it in its aims, and the Globalist regimes that

---

[18] President George Washington's Farewell Address, September 19, 1796.

preceded them were enamored with entangling alliances. They gave aid and comfort to foreign powers hostile to America's national interests, and they worked overtime to denigrate America's history and rich Christian heritage. Despite eight uninterrupted years of achieving every goal on their agenda, The Obama-Biden administration and its allies on the Left in America are still in a state of outrage. And that rage is most visible in the unprecedented attack upon the Constitution. Hillary Clinton, the loser of the 2016, actively encouraged Joe Biden not to concede the 2020 Election, should he be declared the loser. So much for her assertions in 2016 that questioning the outcome of a presidential election would be "un-American!" And so much for the Democrat Party's adherence to the time-honored peaceful transition of political power in America. And they continue to mock President Trump and his followers for demanding election integrity and questioning the election fraud that was so rampant in the 2020 Election. It is the height of hypocrisy.

Barack Hussein Obama and Joe Biden had success at every turn. Whether on ObamaCare, homosexual "marriage," increasing the minimum wage, increasing the national debt, enriching and empowering the fanatical Muslims in Iran and elsewhere, Obama received virtually no opposition from the Republican-led Congress or the Supreme Court. The High Court even violated its duty under the Constitution by supporting Obama's Left-wing radical plan to socialize America's healthcare system, and provided him the excuse to do so.

But despite victory after victory, more Americans became

unemployed, less people had access to adequate, affordable healthcare coverage, more people on food stamps and government assistance, and America's borders less secure and the economy under more debt than ever before. Obama's victories were at the expense of America's livelihood and Constitutional integrity. He instituted the philosophy of his Globalist Socialist heroes and his anti-American pastor under the guise of "Hope and Change," and the end result was bringing America to the brink of extinction as a superpower and great force for good.

And Joe Biden continues the failed policies of the Obama administration, and now enjoys the unfettered support of a Congress controlled by the Democrat Party and a Supreme Court lacking the will to challenge their arguably unlawful, unconstitutional initiatives.

To our south, we see the economic despair and desperation of Venezuela. A once thriving oil-rich economy was reduced to ruin as a testament to Socialist policies. But despite this, Socialist pockets in America elected Left-wing zealots who ignorantly champion Socialism as the pathway to prosperity. They seek to redistribute wealth by taxing hard-working Americans to satisfy their supporters, many of whom are illegals who they actually encourage to vote, in violation of the law. And those who once cried for "tolerance" for their deviant views are now the most intolerant.

And what happens to these Socialist wannabes if society fails to bend to their every whim? Well, they protest, of course, violently, and double down on the bankrupt policies they champion. They, like the community organizers they worship, cry "racism" and "injustice" and demand even more radical change. These children of Obama and the new Democrat Party want even more in taxes taken from American taxpayers to fund their foolishness. They even turn on the radical professors that taught them such anarchy and disrespect. They reap what they have sown.

We see the violent protests of these fascists as they seek to thwart the Movement to Make America Great Again. They seek to defund, eliminate, and even prosecute our law enforcement community. They are the purveyors of anarchy.

And we yearn for a Judicial system worthy of the challenges before us, not judges and justices willing to bend established law to meet the changing winds of public opinion. The Law is an anchor for stability and order in our society, and, as presidents since our Founding Father have proclaimed, the Constitution and the Bible are proper standards that form the foundation of our republic.

In the final analysis, We the People must become the means by which the destruction of America and our Founding Christian Principles are thwarted. Ensuring election integrity and voting out those who have violated their oaths of office are national imperatives. We must ensure that all who would serve in government strictly interpret the Constitution as the Founders intended, and not substitute their will for the Law. We are unique among nations because of God-inspired foundation and national identity. The success of this experiment in republican government depends on an adherence to putting America First. Our future generations will reap the rewards or suffer the consequences of the choices we now make on our conduct as American citizens and who we elect as our political representatives, and knowing who they support as judges and justices in the Judiciary. Let us decide well, having the knowledge and the wisdom to choose wisely.

A wise man will hear, and will increase learning;
and a man of understanding shall attain unto wise counsels:
To understand a proverb, and the interpretation;
the words of the wise, and their dark sayings.

~ Proverbs 1:5-6

During my youth there were many wonderful sayings, now considered trite, that provided cryptic, yet prescient guidance for my life. Among them was one based on Luke 12:48: "To whom much is given of him much is required." Perhaps such sentiments are embarrassing in sophisticated company today, but I continue to believe this with all my heart. I do believe that we are required to wade into those things that matter to our country and our culture, no matter what the disincentives are, and no matter the personal cost. There is not one among us who wants to be set upon, or obligated to do and say difficult things. Yet, there is not one of us who could in good conscience stand by and watch a loved one or a defenseless person—or a vital national principle—perish alone, undefended, when our intervention could make all the difference. This may well be too dramatic an example. But nevertheless, put most simply: if we think that something is dreadfully wrong, then someone has to do something.

~ Justice Clarence Thomas, February 2001

# Chapter 5

# The Declaration of Independence

**July 4, 1776**

## In CONGRESS, July 4, 1776.

**The unanimous Declaration of the thirteen united States of America,**

When in the Course of human events, it becomes necessary for one people to dissolve the political bands which have connected them with another, and to assume among the powers of the earth, the separate and equal station to which the Laws of Nature and of Nature's God entitle them, a decent respect to the opinions of mankind requires that they should declare the causes which impel them to the separation.

We hold these truths to be self-evident, that all men are created equal, that they are endowed by their Creator with certain unalienable Rights, that among these are Life, Liberty and the pursuit of Happiness.--That to secure these rights, Governments are instituted among Men, deriving their just powers from the consent of the governed, --That whenever any Form of Government becomes destructive of these ends, it is the Right of the People to alter or to abolish it, and to institute new Government, laying its foundation on such principles and organizing its powers in such form, as to them shall seem most likely to effect their Safety and Happiness. Prudence, indeed, will dictate that Governments long established should not be changed for light and transient causes; and accordingly all experience hath shewn, that mankind are more disposed to suffer, while evils are sufferable, than to right themselves by abolishing the forms to which they are accustomed. But when a long train of abuses and usurpations, pursuing invariably the same Object evinces a design to reduce them under absolute Despotism, it is their right, it is their duty, to throw off such Government, and to provide new Guards for their future security.--Such has been the patient sufferance of these Colonies; and such is now the necessity which constrains them to alter their former Systems of Government. The history of the present King of Great Britain is a history of repeated injuries and usurpations, all having in direct object the establishment of an absolute Tyranny over these States. To prove this, let Facts be submitted to a candid world.

He has refused his Assent to Laws, the most wholesome and necessary for the public good.

He has forbidden his Governors to pass Laws of immediate and pressing importance, unless suspended in their operation till his Assent should be obtained; and when so suspended, he has utterly neglected to attend to them.

He has refused to pass other Laws for the accommodation of large districts of people, unless those people would relinquish the right of Representation in the Legislature, a right inestimable to them and formidable to tyrants only.

He has called together legislative bodies at places unusual, uncomfortable, and distant from the depository of their public Records, for the sole purpose of fatiguing them into compliance with his measures.

He has dissolved Representative Houses repeatedly, for opposing with manly firmness his invasions on the rights of the people.

He has refused for a long time, after such dissolutions, to cause others to be elected; whereby the Legislative powers, incapable of Annihilation, have returned to the People at large for their exercise; the State remaining in the mean time exposed to all the dangers of invasion from without, and convulsions within.

He has endeavoured to prevent the population of these States; for that purpose obstructing the Laws for Naturalization of Foreigners; refusing to pass others to encourage their migrations hither, and raising the conditions of new Appropriations of Lands.

He has obstructed the Administration of Justice, by refusing his Assent to Laws for establishing Judiciary powers. He has made Judges dependent on his Will alone, for the tenure of their offices, and the amount and payment of their salaries.

He has erected a multitude of New Offices, and sent hither swarms of Officers to harrass our people, and eat out their substance.

He has kept among us, in times of peace, Standing Armies without the Consent of our legislatures.

He has affected to render the Military independent of and superior to the Civil power.

He has combined with others to subject us to a jurisdiction foreign to our constitution, and unacknowledged by our laws; giving his Assent to their Acts of pretended Legislation:

For Quartering large bodies of armed troops among us:

For protecting them, by a mock Trial, from punishment for any Murders which they should commit on the Inhabitants of these States:

For cutting off our Trade with all parts of the world: For imposing Taxes on us without our Consent: For depriving us in many cases, of the benefits of Trial by Jury:

For transporting us beyond Seas to be tried for pretended offences

For abolishing the free System of English Laws in a neighbouring Province, establishing therein an Arbitrary government, and enlarging its Boundaries so as to render it at once an example and fit instrument for introducing the same absolute rule into these Colonies:

For taking away our Charters, abolishing our most valuable Laws, and altering fundamentally the Forms of our Governments:

For suspending our own Legislatures, and declaring themselves invested with power to legislate for us in all cases whatsoever.

He has abdicated Government here, by declaring us out of his Protection and waging War against us.

He has plundered our seas, ravaged our Coasts, burnt our towns, and destroyed the lives of our people.

He is at this time transporting large Armies of foreign Mercenaries to compleat the works of death, desolation and tyranny, already begun with circumstances of Cruelty & perfidy scarcely paralleled in the most barbarous ages, and totally unworthy the Head of a civilized nation.

He has constrained our fellow Citizens taken Captive on the high Seas to bear Arms against their Country, to become the executioners of their friends and Brethren, or to fall themselves by their Hands.

He has excited domestic insurrections amongst us, and has endeavoured to bring on the inhabitants of our frontiers, the merciless Indian Savages, whose known rule of warfare, is an undistinguished destruction of all ages, sexes and conditions.

In every stage of these Oppressions We have Petitioned for Redress in the most humble terms: Our repeated Petitions have been answered only by repeated injury. A Prince whose character is thus marked by every act which may define a Tyrant, is unfit to be the ruler of a free people.

Nor have We been wanting in attentions to our British brethren. We have warned them from time to time of attempts by their legislature to extend an unwarrantable jurisdiction over us. We have reminded them of the circumstances of our emigration and settlement here. We have appealed to their native justice and magnanimity, and we have conjured them by the ties of our common kindred to disavow these usurpations, which, would inevitably interrupt our connections and correspondence. They too have been deaf to the voice of justice and of consanguinity. We must, therefore, acquiesce in the necessity, which denounces our Separation, and hold them, as we hold the rest of mankind, Enemies in War, in Peace Friends.

We, therefore, the Representatives of the united States of America, in General Congress, Assembled, appealing to the Supreme Judge of the world for the rectitude of our intentions, do, in the Name, and by Authority of the good People of these Colonies, solemnly publish and declare, That these United Colonies are, and of Right ought to be Free and Independent States; that they are Absolved from all Allegiance to the British Crown, and that all political connection between them and the State of Great Britain, is and ought to be totally dissolved; and that as Free and Independent States, they have full Power to levy War, conclude Peace, contract Alliances, establish Commerce, and to do all other Acts and Things which Independent States may of right do. And for the support of this Declaration, with a firm reliance on the protection of divine Providence, we mutually pledge to each other our Lives, our Fortunes and our sacred Honor.

**Column 1**
**Georgia:**
  Button Gwinnett
  Lyman Hall
  George Walton

**Column 2**
**North Carolina:**
  William Hooper
  Joseph Hewes
  John Penn
**South Carolina:**
  Edward Rutledge
  Thomas Heyward, Jr.
  Thomas Lynch, Jr.
  Arthur Middleton

**Column 3**
**Massachusetts:**

# John Hancock

**Maryland:**
Samuel Chase
William Paca
Thomas Stone
Charles Carroll of Carrollton
**Virginia:**
George Wythe
Richard Henry Lee
Thomas Jefferson
Benjamin Harrison
Thomas Nelson, Jr.
Francis Lightfoot Lee

Carter Braxton

**Column 4**
**Pennsylvania:**
  Robert Morris
  Benjamin Rush
  Benjamin Franklin
  John Morton
  George Clymer
  James Smith
  George Taylor
  James Wilson
  George Ross
**Delaware:**
  Caesar Rodney
  George Read
  Thomas McKean

**Column 5**
**New York:**
  William Floyd
  Philip Livingston
  Francis Lewis
  Lewis Morris
**New Jersey:**
  Richard Stockton
  John Witherspoon
  Francis Hopkinson
  John Hart
  Abraham Clark

**Column 6**
**New Hampshire:**
  Josiah Bartlett
  William Whipple
**Massachusetts:**
  Samuel Adams

John Adams
Robert Treat Paine
Elbridge Gerry
**Rhode Island:**
Stephen Hopkins
William Ellery
**Connecticut:**
Roger Sherman
Samuel Huntington
William Williams
Oliver Wolcott
**New Hampshire:**
Matthew Thornton

We stand here on the only island of freedom that is left in the whole world. There is no place left to flee to…no place to escape to. We defend freedom here or it is gone. There is no place for us to run, only to make a stand. And if we fail, I think we face telling our children, and our children's children, what it was we found more precious than freedom. Because I am sure that someday — if we fail in this — there will be a generation that will ask.

~ President Ronald Reagan

# Chapter 6

# The United States Constitution

**September 17, 1787**

**(Preamble)**

**W**e the People of the United States, in Order to form a more perfect Union, establish Justice, insure domestic Tranquility, provide for the common defence, promote the general Welfare, and secure the Blessings of Liberty to ourselves and our Posterity, do ordain and establish this Constitution for the United States of America.

## Article I (Article 1 - Legislative)

### Section 1

All legislative Powers herein granted shall be vested in a Congress of the United States, which shall consist of a Senate and House of Representatives.

### Section 2

1: The House of Representatives shall be composed of Members chosen every second Year by the People of the several States, and the Electors in each State shall have the Qualifications requisite for Electors of the most numerous Branch of the State Legislature.

2: No Person shall be a Representative who shall not have attained to the Age of twenty five Years, and been seven Years a Citizen of the United States, and who shall not, when elected, be an Inhabitant of that State in which he shall be chosen.

3: Representatives and direct Taxes shall be apportioned among the several States which may be included within this Union, according to their respective Numbers, which shall be determined by adding to the whole Number of free Persons, including those bound to Service for a Term of Years, and excluding Indians not taxed, three fifths of all other Persons. The actual Enumeration shall be made within three Years after the first Meeting of the Congress of the United States, and within every subsequent Term of ten Years, in such Manner as they shall by Law direct. The Number of Representatives shall not exceed one for every thirty Thousand, but each State shall have at Least one Representative; and until such enumeration shall be made, the State of New Hampshire shall be entitled to chuse three, Massachusetts eight, Rhode-Island and Providence Plantations one, Connecticut five, New-York six, New Jersey four, Pennsylvania eight, Delaware one, Maryland six, Virginia ten, North Carolina five, South Carolina five, and Georgia three.

4: When vacancies happen in the Representation from any State, the Executive Authority thereof shall issue Writs of Election to fill such Vacancies.

5: The House of Representatives shall chuse their Speaker and other Officers; and shall have the sole Power of Impeachment.


## Section 3

1: The Senate of the United States shall be composed of two Senators from each State, chosen by the Legislature thereof,[3] for six Years; and each Senator shall have one Vote.

2: Immediately after they shall be assembled in Consequence of the first Election, they shall be divided as equally as may be into three Classes. The Seats of the Senators of the first Class shall be vacated at the Expiration of the second Year, of the second Class at the Expiration of the fourth Year, and of the third Class at the Expiration of the sixth Year, so that one third may be chosen every second Year; and if Vacancies happen by Resignation, or otherwise, during the Recess of the Legislature of any State, the Executive thereof may make temporary Appointments until the next Meeting of the Legislature, which shall then fill such Vacancies.

3: No Person shall be a Senator who shall not have attained to the Age of thirty Years, and been nine Years a Citizen of the United States, and who shall not, when elected, be an Inhabitant of that State for which he shall be chosen.

4: The Vice President of the United States shall be President of the Senate, but shall have no Vote, unless they be equally divided.

5: The Senate shall chuse their other Officers, and also a President pro tempore, in the Absence of the Vice President, or when he shall exercise the Office of President of the United States.

6: The Senate shall have the sole Power to try all Impeachments. When sitting for that Purpose, they shall be on Oath or Affirmation. When the President of the United States is tried, the Chief Justice shall preside: And no Person shall be convicted without the Concurrence of two thirds of the Members present.

7: Judgment in Cases of impeachment shall not extend further than to removal from Office, and disqualification to hold and enjoy any Office of honor, Trust or Profit under the United States: but the Party convicted shall nevertheless be liable and subject to Indictment, Trial, Judgment and Punishment, according to Law.

**Section 4**

1: The Times, Places and Manner of holding Elections for Senators and Representatives, shall be prescribed in each State by the Legislature thereof; but the Congress may at any time by Law make or alter such Regulations, except as to the Places of chusing Senators.

2: The Congress shall assemble at least once in every Year, and such Meeting shall be on the first Monday in December,[5] unless they shall by Law appoint a different Day.

## Section 5

1: Each House shall be the Judge of the Elections, Returns and Qualifications of its own Members, and a Majority of each shall constitute a Quorum to do Business; but a smaller Number may adjourn from day to day, and may be authorized to compel the Attendance of absent Members, in such Manner, and under such Penalties as each House may provide.

2: Each House may determine the Rules of its Proceedings, punish its Members for disorderly Behaviour, and, with the Concurrence of two thirds, expel a Member.

3: Each House shall keep a Journal of its Proceedings, and from time to time publish the same, excepting such Parts as may in their Judgment require Secrecy; and the Yeas and Nays of the Members of either House on any question shall, at the Desire of one fifth of those Present, be entered on the Journal.

4: Neither House, during the Session of Congress, shall, without the Consent of the other, adjourn for more than three days, nor to any other Place than that in which the two Houses shall be sitting.

## Section 6

1: The Senators and Representatives shall receive a Compensation for their Services, to be ascertained by Law, and paid out of the Treasury of the United States.[6] They shall in all Cases, except Treason, Felony and Breach of the Peace, be privileged from Arrest during their Attendance at the Session of their respective Houses, and in going to and returning from the same; and for any Speech or Debate in either House, they shall not be questioned in any other Place.

2: No Senator or Representative shall, during the Time for which he was elected, be appointed to any civil Office under the Authority of the United States, which shall have been created, or the Emoluments whereof shall have been encreased during such time; and no Person holding any Office under the United States, shall be a Member of either House during his Continuance in Office.

**Section 7**

1: All Bills for raising Revenue shall originate in the House of Representatives; but the Senate may propose or concur with Amendments as on other Bills.

2: Every Bill which shall have passed the House of Representatives and the Senate, shall, before it become a Law, be presented to the President of the United States; If he approve he shall sign it, but if not he shall return it, with his Objections to that House in which it shall have originated, who shall enter the Objections at large on their Journal, and proceed to reconsider it. If after such Reconsideration two thirds of that House shall agree to pass the Bill, it shall be sent, together with the Objections, to the other House, by which it shall likewise be reconsidered, and if approved by two thirds of that House, it shall become a Law. But in all such Cases the Votes of both Houses shall be determined by yeas and Nays, and the Names of the Persons voting for and against the Bill shall be entered on the Journal of each House respectively. If any Bill shall not be returned by the President within ten Days (Sundays excepted) after it shall have been presented to him, the Same shall be a Law, in like Manner as if he had signed it, unless the Congress by their Adjournment prevent its Return, in which Case it shall not be a Law.

3: Every Order, Resolution, or Vote to which the Concurrence of the Senate and House of Representatives may be necessary (except on a question of Adjournment) shall be presented to the President of the United States; and before the Same shall take Effect, shall be approved by him, or being disapproved by him, shall be repassed by two thirds of the Senate and House of Representatives, according to the Rules and Limitations prescribed in the Case of a Bill.

## Section 8

1: The Congress shall have Power To lay and collect Taxes, Duties, Imposts and Excises, to pay the Debts and provide for the common Defence and general Welfare of the United States; but all Duties, Imposts and Excises shall be uniform throughout the United States;

2: To borrow Money on the credit of the United States;

3: To regulate Commerce with foreign Nations, and among the several States, and with the Indian Tribes;

4: To establish an uniform Rule of Naturalization, and uniform Laws on the subject of Bankruptcies throughout the United States;

5: To coin Money, regulate the Value thereof, and of foreign Coin, and fix the Standard of Weights and Measures;

6: To provide for the Punishment of counterfeiting the Securities and current Coin of the United States;

7: To establish Post Offices and post Roads;

8: To promote the Progress of Science and useful Arts, by securing for limited Times to Authors and Inventors the exclusive Right to their respective Writings and Discoveries;

9: To constitute Tribunals inferior to the supreme Court;

10: To define and punish Piracies and Felonies committed on the high Seas, and Offences against the Law of Nations;

11: To declare War, grant Letters of Marque and Reprisal, and make Rules concerning Captures on Land and Water;

12: To raise and support Armies, but no Appropriation of Money to that Use shall be for a longer Term than two Years;

13: To provide and maintain a Navy;

14: To make Rules for the Government and Regulation of the land and naval Forces;

15: To provide for calling forth the Militia to execute the Laws of the Union, suppress Insurrections and repel Invasions;

16: To provide for organizing, arming, and disciplining, the Militia, and for governing such Part of them as may be employed in the Service of the United States, reserving to the States respectively, the Appointment of the Officers, and the Authority of training the Militia according to the discipline prescribed by Congress;

17: To exercise exclusive Legislation in all Cases whatsoever, over such District (not exceeding ten Miles square) as may, by Cession of particular States, and the Acceptance of Congress, become the Seat of the Government of the United States, and to exercise like Authority over all Places purchased by the Consent of the Legislature of the State in which the Same shall be, for the Erection of Forts, Magazines, Arsenals, dock-Yards, and other needful Buildings;—And

18: To make all Laws which shall be necessary and proper for carrying into Execution the foregoing Powers, and all other Powers vested by this Constitution in the Government of the United States, or in any Department or Officer thereof.

## Section 9

1: The Migration or Importation of such Persons as any of the States now existing shall think proper to admit, shall not be prohibited by the Congress prior to the Year one thousand eight hundred and eight, but a Tax or duty may be imposed on such Importation, not exceeding ten dollars for each Person.

2: The Privilege of the Writ of Habeas Corpus shall not be suspended, unless when in Cases of Rebellion or Invasion the public Safety may require it.

3: No Bill of Attainder or ex post facto Law shall be passed.

4: No Capitation, or other direct, Tax shall be laid, unless in Proportion to the Census or Enumeration herein before directed to be taken.

5: No Tax or Duty shall be laid on Articles exported from any State.

6: No Preference shall be given by any Regulation of Commerce or Revenue to the Ports of one State over those of another: nor shall Vessels bound to, or from, one State, be obliged to enter, clear, or pay Duties in another.

7: No Money shall be drawn from the Treasury, but in Consequence of Appropriations made by Law; and a regular

Statement and Account of the Receipts and Expenditures of all public Money shall be published from time to time.

8: No Title of Nobility shall be granted by the United States: And no Person holding any Office of Profit or Trust under them, shall, without the Consent of the Congress, accept of any present, Emolument, Office, or Title, of any kind whatever, from any King, Prince, or foreign State.

## Section 10

1: No State shall enter into any Treaty, Alliance, or Confederation; grant Letters of Marque and Reprisal; coin Money; emit Bills of Credit; make any Thing but gold and silver Coin a Tender in Payment of Debts; pass any Bill of Attainder, ex post facto Law, or Law impairing the Obligation of Contracts, or grant any Title of Nobility.

2: No State shall, without the Consent of the Congress, lay any Imposts or Duties on Imports or Exports, except what may be absolutely necessary for executing it's inspection Laws: and the net Produce of all Duties and Imposts, laid by any State on Imports or Exports, shall be for the Use of the Treasury of the United States; and all such Laws shall be subject to the Revision and Controul of the Congress.

3: No State shall, without the Consent of Congress, lay any Duty of Tonnage, keep Troops, or Ships of War in time of Peace, enter into any Agreement or Compact with another State, or with a foreign Power, or engage in War, unless actually invaded, or in such imminent Danger as will not admit of delay.

# Article II (Article 2 - Executive)

## Section 1

1: The executive Power shall be vested in a President of the United States of America. He shall hold his Office during the Term of four Years, and, together with the Vice President, chosen for the same Term, be elected, as follows

2: Each State shall appoint, in such Manner as the Legislature thereof may direct, a Number of Electors, equal to the whole Number of Senators and Representatives to which the State may be entitled in the Congress: but no Senator or Representative, or Person holding an Office of Trust or Profit under the United States, shall be appointed an Elector.

3: The Electors shall meet in their respective States, and vote by Ballot for two Persons, of whom one at least shall not be an Inhabitant of the same State with themselves. And they shall make a List of all the Persons voted for, and of the Number of Votes for each; which List they shall sign and certify, and transmit sealed to the Seat of the Government of the United States, directed to the President of the Senate. The President of the Senate shall, in the Presence of the Senate and House of Representatives, open all the Certificates, and the Votes shall then be counted. The Person having the greatest Number of Votes shall be the President, if such Number be a Majority of the whole Number of Electors appointed; and if there be more than one who have such Majority, and have an equal Number of Votes, then the House of Representatives shall immediately chuse by Ballot one of them for President; and if no Person have a Majority, then from the five highest on the List the said House shall in like Manner chuse the President. But in chusing the President, the Votes shall be taken by States, the Representation from each State having one Vote; A quorum for this Purpose shall consist of a Member or Members from two thirds of the States, and a Majority of all the States shall be necessary to a Choice. In every Case, after the Choice of the President, the Person having the greatest Number of Votes of the Electors shall be the Vice President. But if there should remain two or more who have equal Votes, the Senate shall chuse from them by Ballot the Vice President.

4: The Congress may determine the Time of chusing the Electors, and the Day on which they shall give their Votes; which Day shall be the same throughout the United States.

5: No Person except a natural born Citizen, or a Citizen of the United States, at the time of the Adoption of this Constitution, shall be eligible to the Office of President; neither shall any Person be eligible to that Office who shall not have attained to the Age of thirty five Years, and been fourteen Years a Resident within the United States.

6: In Case of the Removal of the President from Office, or of his Death, Resignation, or Inability to discharge the Powers and Duties of the said Office,  the Same shall devolve on the VicePresident, and the Congress may by Law provide for the Case of Removal, Death, Resignation or Inability, both of the President and Vice President, declaring what Officer shall then act as President, and such Officer shall act accordingly, until the Disability be removed, or a President shall be elected.

7: The President shall, at stated Times, receive for his Services, a Compensation, which shall neither be encreased nor diminished during the Period for which he shall have been elected, and he shall not receive within that Period any other Emolument from the United States, or any of them.

8: Before he enter on the Execution of his Office, he shall take the following Oath or Affirmation: — "I do solemnly swear (or affirm) that I will faithfully execute the Office of President of the United States, and will to the best of my Ability, preserve, protect and defend the Constitution of the United States."

## Section 2

1: The President shall be Commander in Chief of the Army and Navy of the United States, and of the Militia of the several States, when called into the actual Service of the United States; he may require the Opinion, in writing, of the principal Officer in each of the executive Departments, upon any Subject relating to the Duties of their respective Offices, and he shall have Power to grant Reprieves and Pardons for Offences against the United States, except in Cases of Impeachment.

2: He shall have Power, by and with the Advice and Consent of the Senate, to make Treaties, provided two thirds of the Senators present concur; and he shall nominate, and by and with the Advice and Consent of the Senate, shall appoint Ambassadors, other public Ministers and Consuls, Judges of the supreme Court, and all other Officers of the United States, whose Appointments are not herein otherwise provided for, and which shall be established by Law: but the Congress may by Law vest the Appointment of such inferior Officers, as they think proper, in the President alone, in the Courts of Law, or in the Heads of Departments.

3: The President shall have Power to fill up all Vacancies that may happen during the Recess of the Senate, by granting Commissions which shall expire at the End of their next Session.

## Section 3

He shall from time to time give to the Congress Information of the State of the Union, and recommend to their Consideration such Measures as he shall judge necessary and expedient; he may, on extraordinary Occasions, convene both Houses, or either of them, and in Case of Disagreement between them, with Respect to the Time of Adjournment, he may adjourn them to such Time as he shall think proper; he shall receive Ambassadors and other public Ministers; he shall take Care that the Laws be faithfully executed, and shall Commission all the Officers of the United States.

## Section 4

The President, Vice President and all civil Officers of the United States, shall be removed from Office on Impeachment for, and Conviction of, Treason, Bribery, or other high Crimes and Misdemeanors.

# Article III (Article 3 - Judicial)

## Section 1

The judicial Power of the United States, shall be vested in one supreme Court, and in such inferior Courts as the Congress may from time to time ordain and establish. The Judges, both of the supreme and inferior Courts, shall hold their Offices during good Behaviour, and shall, at stated Times, receive for their Services, a Compensation, which shall not be diminished during their Continuance in Office.

## Section 2

1: The judicial Power shall extend to all Cases, in Law and Equity, arising under this Constitution, the Laws of the United States, and Treaties made, or which shall be made, under their Authority;—to all Cases affecting Ambassadors, other public Ministers and Consuls;—to all Cases of admiralty and maritime Jurisdiction;—to Controversies to which the United States shall be a Party;—to Controversies between two or more States;—between a State and Citizens of another State; —between Citizens of different States, —between Citizens of the same State claiming Lands under Grants of different States, and between a State, or the Citizens thereof, and foreign States, Citizens or Subjects.

2: In all Cases affecting Ambassadors, other public Ministers and Consuls, and those in which a State shall be Party, the supreme Court shall have original Jurisdiction. In all the other Cases before mentioned, the supreme Court shall have appellate Jurisdiction, both as to Law and Fact, with such Exceptions, and under such Regulations as the Congress shall make.

3: The Trial of all Crimes, except in Cases of Impeachment, shall be by Jury; and such Trial shall be held in the State where the said Crimes shall have been committed; but when not committed within any State, the Trial shall be at such Place or Places as the Congress may by Law have directed.

## Section 3

1: Treason against the United States, shall consist only in levying War against them, or in adhering to their Enemies, giving them Aid and Comfort. No Person shall be convicted of

Treason unless on the Testimony of two Witnesses to the same overt Act, or on Confession in open Court.

2: The Congress shall have Power to declare the Punishment of Treason, but no Attainder of Treason shall work Corruption of Blood, or Forfeiture except during the Life of the Person attainted.

## Article IV (Article 4 - States' Relations)

### Section 1

Full Faith and Credit shall be given in each State to the public Acts, Records, and judicial Proceedings of every other State. And the Congress may by general Laws prescribe the Manner in which such Acts, Records and Proceedings shall be proved, and the Effect thereof.

### Section 2

1: The Citizens of each State shall be entitled to all Privileges and Immunities of Citizens in the several States.

2: A Person charged in any State with Treason, Felony, or other Crime, who shall flee from Justice, and be found in another State, shall on Demand of the executive Authority of the State from which he fled, be delivered up, to be removed to the State having Jurisdiction of the Crime.

3: No Person held to Service or Labour in one State, under the Laws thereof, escaping into another, shall, in Consequence of any Law or Regulation therein, be discharged from such

Service or Labour, but shall be delivered up on Claim of the Party to whom such Service or Labour may be due.

### Section 3

1: New States may be admitted by the Congress into this Union; but no new State shall be formed or erected within the Jurisdiction of any other State; nor any State be formed by the Junction of two or more States, or Parts of States, without the Consent of the Legislatures of the States concerned as well as of the Congress.

2: The Congress shall have Power to dispose of and make all needful Rules and Regulations respecting the Territory or other Property belonging to the United States; and nothing in this Constitution shall be so construed as to Prejudice any Claims of the United States, or of any particular State.

### Section 4

The United States shall guarantee to every State in this Union a Republican Form of Government, and shall protect each of them against Invasion; and on Application of the Legislature, or of the Executive (when the Legislature cannot be convened) against domestic Violence.

### Article V (Article 5 - Mode of Amendment)

The Congress, whenever two thirds of both Houses shall deem it necessary, shall propose **Amendments** to this Constitution, or, on the Application of the Legislatures of two thirds of the several States, shall call a Convention for proposing Amendments, which, in either Case, shall be valid to all Intents and Purposes, as Part of this Constitution, when ratified by the Legislatures of three fourths of the several States, or by Conventions in three fourths thereof, as the one or the other Mode of Ratification may be proposed by the Congress; Provided that no Amendment which may be made prior to the Year One thousand eight hundred and eight shall in any Manner affect the first and fourth Clauses in the Ninth Section of the first Article; and that no State, without its Consent, shall be deprived of its equal Suffrage in the Senate.

## Article VI (Article 6 - Prior Debts, National Supremacy, Oaths of Offic)

1: All Debts contracted and Engagements entered into, before the Adoption of this Constitution, shall be as valid against the United States under this Constitution, as under the Confederation.

2: This Constitution, and the Laws of the United States which shall be made in Pursuance thereof; and all Treaties made, or which shall be made, under the Authority of the United States, shall be the supreme Law of the Land; and the Judges in every State shall be bound thereby, any Thing in the Constitution or Laws of any State to the Contrary notwithstanding.

3: The Senators and Representatives before mentioned, and the Members of the several State Legislatures, and all executive and judicial Officers, both of the United States and of the several States, shall be bound by Oath or Affirmation, to support this Constitution; but no religious Test shall ever be required as a Qualification to any Office or public Trust under the United States.

## Article VII (Article 7 - Ratification)

The Ratification of the Conventions of nine States, shall be sufficient for the Establishment of this Constitution between the States so ratifying the Same.

The Word "the", being interlined between the seventh and eight Lines of the first Page, The Word "Thirty" being partly written on an Erazure in the fifteenth Line of the first Page. The Words "is tried" being interlined between the thirty second and thirty third Lines of the first Page and the Word "the" being interlined between the forty third and forty fourth Lines of the second Page.

**done** in Convention by the Unanimous Consent of the States present the Seventeenth Day of September in the Year of our Lord one thousand seven hundred and Eighty seven and of the Independence of the United States of America the Twelfth **In witness** whereof We have hereunto subscribed our Names,

Attest
William
Jackson
Secretary

G°: Washington -Presid^t. and deputy from Virginia

Delaware

Geo: Read
Gunning Bedford jun
John Dickinson
Richard Bassett
Jaco: Broom

Maryland

James M^cHenry
Dan of S^t   Tho^s. Jenifer
Dan^l Carroll.


Virginia

John Blair —
James Madison Jr.


North Carolina

W^m Blount
Rich^d. Dobbs Spaight.
Hu Williamson


South Carolina

J. Rutledge
Charles Cotesworth Pinckney
Charle_s _Pinckney
Pierce Butler.


Georgia

William Few
Abr Baldwin


New Hampshire

John Langdon
Nicholas Gilman


Massachusetts

Nathaniel Gorham
Rufus King

Connecticut

W$^m$.  Sam$^l$. Johnson
Roger Sherman

New York

Alexander Hamilton

New Jersey

Wil. Livingston
David Brearley.
W$^m$. Paterson.
Jona: Dayton

Pennsylvania

B Franklin
Thomas Mifflin
Rob$^t$ Morris
Geo. Clymer
Tho$^s$. FitzSimons
Jared Ingersoll
James Wilson.
Gouv Morris

## Letter of Transmittal

**In Convention**. Monday September 17th 1787.

Present
The States of

New Hampshire, Massachusetts, Connecticut, Mr. Hamilton
from New York, New Jersey, Pennsylvania, Delaware,

Maryland, Virginia, North Carolina, South Carolina and Georgia.

**Resolved**, That the preceeding Constitution be laid before the United States in Congress assembled, and that it is the Opinion of this Convention, that it should afterwards be submitted to a Convention of Delegates, chosen in each State by the People thereof, under the Recommendation of its Legislature, for their Assent and Ratification; and that each Convention assenting to, and ratifying the Same, should give Notice thereof to the United States in Congress assembled. Resolved, That it is the Opinion of this Convention, that as soon as the Conventions of nine States shall have ratified this Constitution, the United States in Congress assembled should fix a Day on which Electors should be appointed by the States which shall have ratified the same, and a Day on which the Electors should assemble to vote for the President, and the Time and Place for commencing Proceedings under this Constitution.

That after such Publication the Electors should be appointed, and the Senators and Representatives elected: That the Electors should meet on the Day fixed for the Election of the President, and should transmit their Votes certified, signed, sealed and directed, as the Constitution requires, to the Secretary of the United States in Congress assembled, that the Senators and Representatives should convene at the Time and Place assigned; that the Senators should appoint a President of the Senate, for the sole Purpose of receiving, opening and counting the Votes for President; and, that after he shall be chosen, the Congress, together with the President, should, without Delay, proceed to execute this Constitution.

By the unanimous Order of the

Convention

W. Jackson  Secretary. G⁰: Washington -Presidᵗ.

---

**Letter of Transmittal to the President of Congress**

**In Convention**. Monday September 17th 1787.

SIR:

We have now the honor to submit to the consideration of the United States in Congress assembled, that Constitution which has appeared to us the most advisable.

The friends of our country have long seen and desired that the power of making war, peace, and treaties, that of levying money, and regulating commerce, and the correspondent executive and judicial authorities, should be fully and effectually vested in the General Government of the Union; but the impropriety of delegating such extensive trust to one body of men is evident: hence results the necessity of a different organization.

It is obviously impracticable in the Federal Government of these States to secure all rights of independent sovereignty to each, and yet provide for the interest and safety of all. Individuals entering into society must give up a share of liberty to preserve the rest. The magnitude of the sacrifice must depend as well on situation and circumstance, as on the object to be obtained. It is at all times difficult to draw with precision the line between those rights which must be surrendered, and those which may be preserved; and, on the present occasion, this difficulty was increased by a difference among the several States as to their situation, extent, habits, and particular interests.

In all our deliberations on this subject, we kept steadily in our view that which appears to us the greatest interest of every true American, the consolidation of our Union, in which is involved our prosperity, felicity, safety — perhaps our national existence. This important consideration, seriously and deeply impressed on our minds, led each State in the Convention to be less rigid on points of inferior magnitude than might have been otherwise expected; and thus, the Constitution which we now present is the result of a spirit of amity, and of that mutual deference and concession, which the peculiarity of our political situation rendered indispensable.

That it will meet the full and entire approbation of every State is not, perhaps, to be expected; but each will, doubtless, consider, that had her interest alone been consulted, the consequences might have been particularly disagreeable or injurious to others; that it is liable to as few exceptions as could reasonably have been expected, we hope and believe; that it may promote the lasting welfare of that Country so dear to us all, and secure her freedom and happiness, is our most ardent wish.

With great respect, we have the honor to be,

*SIR*, your excellency's most obedient and

humble servants:

GEORGE WASHINGTON, *President.*

*By the unanimous order of the convention.*

His Excellency the President of Congress.

## Amendments to the Constitution

(The procedure for changing the United States Constitution is **Article V** - Mode of Amendment)

(The Preamble to The Bill of Rights)

## Congress OF THE United States

begun and held at the City of New-York, on Wednesday the fourth of March, one thousand seven hundred and eighty nine.

**THE** Conventions of a number of the States, having at the time of their adopting the Constitution, expressed a desire, in order to prevent misconstruction or abuse of its powers, that further declaratory and restrictive clauses should be added: And as extending the ground of public confidence in the Government, will best ensure the beneficent ends of its institution.

**RESOLVED** by the Senate and House of Representatives of the United States of America, in Congress assembled, two thirds of both Houses concurring, that the following Articles be proposed to the Legislatures of the several States, as amendments to the Constitution of the United States, all, or any of which Articles, when ratified by three fourths of the said Legislatures, to be valid to all intents and purposes, as part of the said Constitution; viz.

**ARTICLES** in addition to, and Amendment of the **Constitution of the United States of America**, proposed by Congress, and ratified by the Legislatures of the several States, pursuant to the fifth Article of the original Constitution.

(Articles I through X are known as the Bill of Rights)

-

*Article the first. ....* After the first enumeration required by the first Article of the Constitution, there shall be one Representative for every thirty thousand, until the number shall amount to one hundred, after which, the proportion shall be so regulated by Congress, that there shall be not less than one hundred Representatives, nor less than one Representative for every forty thousand persons, until the number of Representatives shall amount to two hundred, after which the proportion shall be so regulated by Congress, that there shall not be less than two hundred Representatives, nor more than one Representative for every fifty thousand persons.

-

*Article the second. ....* No law, varying the compensation for the services of the Senators and Representatives, shall take effect, until an election of Representatives shall have intervened.

## Article [I] (Amendment 1 - Freedom of expression and religion)

Congress shall make no law respecting an establishment of religion, or prohibiting the free exercise thereof; or abridging the freedom of speech, or of the press; or the right of the people peaceably to assemble, and to petition the Government for a redress of grievances.

## Article [II] (Amendment 2 - Bearing Arms)

A well regulated Militia, being necessary to the security of a free State, the right of the people to keep and bear Arms, shall not be infringed.

## Article [III] (Amendment 3 - Quartering Soldiers)

No Soldier shall, in time of peace be quartered in any house, without the consent of the Owner, nor in time of war, but in a manner to be prescribed by law.

## Article [IV] (Amendment 4 - Search and Seizure)

The right of the people to be secure in their persons, houses, papers, and effects, against unreasonable searches and seizures, shall not be violated, and no Warrants shall issue, but upon probable cause, supported by Oath or affirmation, and particularly describing the place to be searched, and the persons or things to be seized.

## Article [V] (Amendment 5 - Rights of Persons)

No person shall be held to answer for a capital, or otherwise infamous crime, unless on a presentment or indictment of a Grand Jury, except in cases arising in the land or naval forces, or in the Militia, when in actual service in time of War or public danger; nor shall any person be subject for the same offence to be twice put in jeopardy of life or limb; nor shall be compelled in any criminal case to be a witness against himself, nor be deprived of life, liberty, or property, without due process of law; nor shall private property be taken for public use, without just compensation.

## Article [VI] (Amendment 6 - Rights of Accused in Criminal Prosecutions)

In all criminal prosecutions, the accused shall enjoy the right to a speedy and public trial, by an impartial jury of the State and district wherein the crime shall have been committed, which district shall have been previously ascertained by law, and to be informed of the nature and cause of the accusation; to be confronted with the witnesses against him; to have compulsory process for obtaining witnesses in his favor, and to have the Assistance of Counsel for his defence.

## Article [VII] (Amendment 7 - Civil Trials)

In Suits at common law, where the value in controversy shall exceed twenty dollars, the right of trial by jury shall be preserved, and no fact tried by a jury, shall be otherwise re-examined in any Court of the United States, than according to the rules of the common law.

## Article [VIII] (Amendment 8 - Further Guarantees in Criminal Cases)

Excessive bail shall not be required, nor excessive fines imposed, nor cruel and unusual punishments inflicted.

## Article [IX] (Amendment 9 - Unenumerated Rights)

The enumeration in the **Constitution**, of certain rights, shall not be construed to deny or disparage others retained by the people.

## Article [X] (Amendment 10 - Reserved Powers)

The powers not delegated to the United States by the Constitution, nor prohibited by it to the States, are reserved to the States respectively, or to the people.

Attest,
John Beckley, Clerk of the House of Representatives.
Sam. A. Otis Secretary of the Senate.

Frederick Augustus Muhlenberg Speaker of the House of Representatives.
John Adams, Vice-President of the United States, and President of the Senate.

*(end of the Bill of Rights)*

## [Article XI] (Amendment 11 - Suits Against States)

The Judicial power of the United States shall not be construed to extend to any suit in law or equity, commenced or prosecuted against one of the United States by Citizens of another State, or by Citizens or Subjects of any Foreign State.

# [Article XII] (Amendment 12 - Election of President)

The Electors shall meet in their respective states, and vote by ballot for President and Vice-President, one of whom, at least, shall not be an inhabitant of the same state with themselves; they shall name in their ballots the person voted for as President, and in distinct ballots the person voted for as Vice-President, and they shall make distinct lists of all persons voted for as President, and of all persons voted for as Vice-President, and of the number of votes for each, which lists they shall sign and certify, and transmit sealed to the seat of the government of the United States, directed to the President of the Senate;—The President of the Senate shall, in the presence of the Senate and House of Representatives, open all the certificates and the votes shall then be counted;—The person having the greatest number of votes for President, shall be the President, if such number be a majority of the whole number of Electors appointed; and if no person have such majority, then from the persons having the highest numbers not exceeding three on the list of those voted for as President, the House of Representatives shall choose immediately, by ballot, the President. But in choosing the President, the votes shall be taken by states, the representation from each state having one vote; a quorum for this purpose shall consist of a member or members from two-thirds of the states, and a majority of all the states shall be necessary to a choice. And if the House of Representatives shall not choose a President whenever the right of choice shall devolve upon them, before the fourth day of March next following, then the Vice-President shall act as President, as in the case of the death or other constitutional disability of the President. —The person having the greatest number of votes as Vice-President, shall be the Vice-President, if such number be a majority of the whole number of Electors appointed, and if no person have a majority, then from the two highest numbers on the list, the Senate shall choose the Vice-President; a quorum for the purpose shall consist of two-thirds of the whole number of Senators, and a majority of the whole number shall be necessary to a choice. But no person constitutionally ineligible to the office of President shall be eligible to that of Vice-President of the United States.

## Article XIII (Amendment 13 - Slavery and Involuntary Servitude)

Neither slavery nor involuntary servitude, except as a punishment for crime whereof the party shall have been duly convicted, shall exist within the United States, or any place subject to their jurisdiction.

Congress shall have power to enforce this article by appropriate legislation.

## Article XIV (Amendment 14 - Rights Guaranteed: Privileges and Immunities of Citizenship, Due Process, and Equal Protection)

1: All persons born or naturalized in the United States, and subject to the jurisdiction thereof, are citizens of the United States and of the State wherein they reside. No State shall make or enforce any law which shall abridge the privileges or immunities of citizens of the United States; nor shall any State deprive any person of life, liberty, or property, without due process of law; nor deny to any person within its jurisdiction the equal protection of the laws.

2: Representatives shall be apportioned among the several States according to their respective numbers, counting the whole number of persons in each State, excluding Indians not taxed. But when the right to vote at any election for the choice of electors for President and Vice President of the United States, Representatives in Congress, the Executive and Judicial officers of a State, or the members of the Legislature thereof, is denied to any of the male inhabitants of such State, being twenty-one years of age,[15] and citizens of the United States, or in any way abridged, except for participation in rebellion, or other crime, the basis of representation therein shall be reduced in the proportion which the number of such male citizens shall bear to the whole number of male citizens twenty-one years of age in such State.

3: No person shall be a Senator or Representative in Congress, or elector of President and Vice President, or hold any office, civil or military, under the United States, or under any State, who, having previously taken an oath, as a member of Congress, or as an officer of the United States, or as a member of any State legislature, or as an executive or judicial officer of any State, to support the Constitution of the United States, shall have engaged in insurrection or rebellion against the same, or given aid or comfort to the enemies thereof. But Congress may by a vote of two-thirds of each House, remove such disability.

4: The validity of the public debt of the United States, authorized by law, including debts incurred for payment of pensions and bounties for services in suppressing insurrection or rebellion, shall not be questioned. But neither the United States nor any State shall assume or pay any debt or obligation incurred in aid of insurrection or rebellion against the United States, or any claim for the loss or emancipation of any slave; but all such debts, obligations and claims shall be held illegal and void.

5: The Congress shall have power to enforce, by appropriate legislation, the provisions of this article.

## Article XV (Amendment 15 - Rights of Citizens to Vote)

The right of citizens of the United States to vote shall not be denied or abridged by the United States or by any State on account of race, color, or previous condition of servitude.

The Congress shall have power to enforce this article by appropriate legislation.

## Article XVI (Amendment 16 - Income Tax)

The Congress shall have power to lay and collect taxes on incomes, from whatever source derived, without apportionment among the several States, and without regard to any census or enumeration.

## [Article XVII] (Amendment 17 - Popular Election of Senators)

1: The Senate of the United States shall be composed of two Senators from each State, elected by the people thereof, for six years; and each Senator shall have one vote. The electors in each State shall have the qualifications requisite for electors of the most numerous branch of the State legislatures.

2: When vacancies happen in the representation of any State in the Senate, the executive authority of such State shall issue writs of election to fill such vacancies: Provided, That the legislature of any State may empower the executive thereof to make temporary appointments until the people fill the vacancies by election as the legislature may direct.

3: This amendment shall not be so construed as to affect the election or term of any Senator chosen before it becomes valid as part of the Constitution.

## Article [XVIII] (Amendment 18 - Prohibition of Intoxicating Liquors)

1: After one year from the ratification of this article the manufacture, sale, or transportation of intoxicating liquors within, the importation thereof into, or the exportation thereof from the United States and all territory subject to the jurisdiction thereof for beverage purposes is hereby prohibited.

2: The Congress and the several States shall have concurrent power to enforce this article by appropriate legislation.

3: This article shall be inoperative unless it shall have been ratified as an amendment to the Constitution by the legislatures of the several States, as provided in the Constitution, within seven years from the date of the submission hereof to the States by the Congress.

## Article [XIX] (Amendment 19 - Women's Suffrage Rights)

The right of citizens of the United States to vote shall not be denied or abridged by the United States or by any State on account of sex.

Congress shall have power to enforce this article by appropriate legislation.

## Article [XX] (Amendment 20 - Terms of President, Vice President, Members of Congress: Presidential Vacancy)

1: The terms of the President and Vice President shall end at noon on the 20th day of January, and the terms of Senators and Representatives at noon on the 3d day of January, of the years in which such terms would have ended if this article had not been ratified; and the terms of their successors shall then begin.

2: The Congress shall assemble at least once in every year, and such meeting shall begin at noon on the 3d day of January, unless they shall by law appoint a different day.

3: If, at the time fixed for the beginning of the term of the President, the President elect shall have died, the Vice President elect shall become President. If a President shall not have been chosen before the time fixed for the beginning of his term, or if the President elect shall have failed to qualify, then the Vice President elect shall act as President until a President shall have qualified; and the Congress may by law provide for the case wherein neither a President elect nor a Vice President elect shall have qualified, declaring who shall then act as President, or the manner in which one who is to act shall be selected, and such person shall act accordingly until a President or Vice President shall have qualified.

4: The Congress may by law provide for the case of the death of any of the persons from whom the House of Representatives may choose a President whenever the right of choice shall have devolved upon them, and for the case of the death of any of the persons from whom the Senate may choose a Vice President whenever the right of choice shall have devolved upon them.

5: Sections 1 and 2 shall take effect on the 15th day of October following the ratification of this article.

6: This article shall be inoperative unless it shall have been ratified as an amendment to the Constitution by the legislatures of three-fourths of the several States within seven years from the date of its submission.

## Article [XXI] (Amendment 21 - Repeal of Eighteenth Amendment)

1: The eighteenth article of amendment to the Constitution of the United States is hereby repealed.

2: The transportation or importation into any State, Territory, or possession of the United States for delivery or use therein of intoxicating liquors, in violation of the laws thereof, is hereby prohibited.

3: This article shall be inoperative unless it shall have been ratified as an amendment to the Constitution by conventions in the several States, as provided in the Constitution, within seven years from the date of the submission hereof to the States by the Congress.

## Amendment XXII (Amendment 22 - Presidential Tenure)

1: No person shall be elected to the office of the President more than twice, and no person who has held the office of President, or acted as President, for more than two years of a term to which some other person was elected President shall be elected to the office of the President more than once. But this article shall not apply to any person holding the office of President when this article was proposed by the Congress, and shall not prevent any person who may be holding the office of President, or acting as President, during the term within which this article becomes operative from holding the office of President or acting as President during the remainder of such term.

2: This article shall be inoperative unless it shall have been ratified as an amendment to the Constitution by the legislatures of three-fourths of the several states within seven years from the date of its submission to the states by the Congress.

## Amendment XXIII (Amendment 23 - Presidential Electors for the District of Columbia)

1: The District constituting the seat of government of the United States shall appoint in such manner as the Congress may direct: A number of electors of President and Vice President equal to the whole number of Senators and Representatives in Congress to which the District would be entitled if it were a state, but in no event more than the least populous state; they shall be in addition to those appointed by the states, but they shall be considered, for the purposes of the election of President and Vice President, to be electors appointed by a state; and they shall meet in the District and perform such duties as provided by the twelfth article of amendment.

2: The Congress shall have power to enforce this article by appropriate legislation.

## Amendment XXIV (Amendment 24 - Abolition of the Poll Tax Qualification in Federal Elections)

1. The right of citizens of the United States to vote in any primary or other election for President or Vice President, for electors for President or Vice President, or for Senator or

Representative in Congress, shall not be denied or abridged by the United States or any state by reason of failure to pay any poll tax or other tax.

2. The Congress shall have power to enforce this article by appropriate legislation.

## Amendment XXV  (Amendment 25 - Presidential Vacancy, Disability, and Inability)

1: In case of the removal of the President from office or of his death or resignation, the Vice President shall become President.

2: Whenever there is a vacancy in the office of the Vice President, the President shall nominate a Vice President who shall take office upon confirmation by a majority vote of both Houses of Congress.

3: Whenever the President transmits to the President pro tempore of the Senate and the Speaker of the House of Representatives his written declaration that he is unable to discharge the powers and duties of his office, and until he transmits to them a written declaration to the contrary, such powers and duties shall be discharged by the Vice President as Acting President.

4: Whenever the Vice President and a majority of either the principal officers of the executive departments or of such other body as Congress may by law provide, transmit to the President pro tempore of the Senate and the Speaker of the House of Representatives their written declaration that the President is unable to discharge the powers and duties of his office, the Vice President shall immediately assume the powers and duties of the office as Acting President.

Thereafter, when the President transmits to the President pro tempore of the Senate and the Speaker of the House of Representatives his written declaration that no inability exists, he shall resume the powers and duties of his office unless the Vice President and a majority of either the principal officers of the executive department or of such other body as Congress may by law provide, transmit within four days to the President pro tempore of the Senate and the Speaker of the House of Representatives their written declaration that the President is unable to discharge the powers and duties of his office. Thereupon Congress shall decide the issue, assembling within forty-eight hours for that purpose if not in session. If the Congress, within twenty-one days after receipt of the latter written declaration, or, if Congress is not in session, within twenty-one days after Congress is required to assemble, determines by two-thirds vote of both Houses that the President is unable to discharge the powers and duties of his office, the Vice President shall continue to discharge the same as Acting President; otherwise, the President shall resume the powers and duties of his office.

## Amendment XXVI (Amendment 26 - Reduction of Voting Age Qualification)

1: The right of citizens of the United States, who are 18 years of age or older, to vote, shall not be denied or abridged by the United States or any state on account of age.

2: The Congress shall have the power to enforce this article by appropriate legislation.

## Amendment XXVII (Amendment 27 - Congressional Pay Limitation)

No law varying the compensation for the services of the Senators and Representatives shall take effect until an election of Representatives shall have intervened.

Freedom is never more than one generation away from extinction. We didn't pass it to our children in the bloodstream. It must be fought for, protected, and handed on for them to do the same, or one day we will spend our sunset years telling our children and our children's children what it was once like in the United States where men were free.

~ President Ronald Reagan

# Conclusion

# Standing in the Gap for America

Standing, as it were in the midst of falling empires, it should be our aim to assume a station and attitude, which will preserve us from being overwhelmed in their ruins.

~ President George Washington,
To the Secretary of War, December 13, 1798

This story shall the good man teach his son; And Crispin Crispian shall ne'er go by, From this day to the ending of the world, But we in it shall be remembered, — We few, we happy few, we band of brothers; For he to-day that sheds his blood with me Shall be my brother; be he ne'er so vile, This day shall gentle his condition: And gentlemen in England now a-bed Shall think themselves accurs'd they were not here, And hold their manhoods cheap while any speaks That fought with us upon Saint Crispin's day.

~ Shakespeare, King Henry V, Act IV, Scene III

In the waning days of the British Empire, soldiers and knights sworn to the cause, before they departed on what could have very well been their final Quest, parted company with a simple saying: "I'll see you at sundown." They, better than most, knew that a cancer was spreading throughout the empire, and the day was fast approaching when men of honor would be left alone to stand in the gap. And one fateful day, just before the end, they would stand shoulder to shoulder in a last ditch effort to stem the tide, that is, to stop the sun from setting on that once-great institution, which contributed so greatly to the culture of Western Civilization, the British Empire.

America has been bankrupted by the corrupt politicians and Deep State partisans that have perfected the art of slander, election fraud, and erosion of confidence in our republic. And when we combined that with the persistent onslaught of pandemics emanating from Communist China against the West to effectively undermine our economy and target our Constitutional representatives for defeat, then we realize Pax Americana is over. The peace we enjoyed has been squandered by a great many politicians, media types, and foreign actors hostile to our way of life. And here I blame not only the Democrat and Republican establishment politicians, but I blame the members of the Judiciary as well. They have forsaken their duty under the Constitution and their oaths to

God and the American people. It is now time for another generation of Americans, outsiders if you will, to enter the arena and repair the damage, and reclaim the promise of America.

But it must be understood that an end the Pax Americana is not necessarily an end to America as a world superpower and a force for good. The events that brought about an end to Greece and Rome and finally Great Britain as dominate world forces for good need not spell America's downfall. There is still time, but that precious time is dwindling.

America has many problems, but we have a great many more blessings. We have it within our power to avoid the fates that befell other great powers like Greece, Rome, and Great Britain. We need to preserve our history and learn from it. The cities of Sodom and Gomorrah were destroyed because they lacked the presence of just ten righteous men.[19] I believe that men and women of courage and good will can change the course of American history for the better. We can change the course of American history! And in case you have any doubts, I am talking about YOU!

I believe in America! I believe God is the author of the American experience and our salvation. We are here not as the product of some evolutionary quirk of science, but as part of a great and divine plan to do good. We were perfectly placed here at this time in the history of the world to make a difference. I believed that of President Trump as well. God

---

[19] 18 Genesis 16-33; 19 Genesis 1-29.

used him in a mighty way. Donald Trump, like Ronald Reagan and others before him in American history, set the example to make America great again, but they could not do it alone! It takes more. And it will take the concerned efforts of good men and women to join this Movement, and propel America positively into the future.

But as I alluded to earlier, even as rich and as powerful as Donald J. Trump may be, his message was infinitely greater! The power of the presidency rests not in wealth or personal power, it rests in the ability to positively influence others. That's called leadership! President Trump effectively used the Bully Pulpit to affect change by providing a vision for our citizens to rally around, and he appointed cabinet members to implement that vision, and he appointed members of the federal judiciary to uphold the strict letter of the Constitution. Donald Trump was a great American President!

I dare say President Obama did not subscribe to that Founding Principle, neither does Joe Biden. Obama used the Bully Pulpit to divide America racially, politically and economically, and he used it as a platform to incite the lowest form of inhabitants in our land to riot and wage war against our law enforcement community. He also appointed lawyers to the federal judiciary that perverted the Constitution and made their will the law. This is Obama's legacy, and Biden is following in his footsteps.

Nevertheless, we can fulfill Presidents Reagan and Trump's vision that "America's best days are yet to come!" But it bears keeping in mind that there will be trials along the way. As the

Good Book, particularly the Book of Psalms, proclaims, we learn more from our valley experiences than we do at the hilltops. My friends, we have spent many years in the valley, and now we entered a *Long Dark Winter*. Let us rise to the occasion and march out of this season and toward the top of the hill. We can do this starting at this very moment, by making a commitment to be the change we seek, and we can change our political leadership in Congress and locally in the 2022 elections. The forces of darkness are great, but God is greater!

We must each in our own way labor to make America great again, adhering to our Founding Christian Principles, which are sown in the very fabric our Declaration of Independence and the Constitution! As Psalm 127:1 states, "Except the LORD build the house, they labour in vain that build it: except the LORD keep the city, the watchman waketh but in vain." We need to rebuild America with a healthy reverence for our Creator and respect for the Rule of Law. It is here that our Judiciary plays no small part. Judges and Justices are the keepers of the Law, and a constitutional check on the powers of the President and Congress.

Remember, Standing in the Gap for America, as well as *Making America Great Again,* requires the embodiment of the same mindset and work ethic that made America great to begin with. Truth, Justice, a reverence to God and our country's Founding Christian Principles, and the vision and good deeds to see them through. This includes voting for champions of America's Founding Christian Principles, whether they be the president, or governors, judges, legislators, mayors, city council or school board members.

Again, so there is no doubt, and as I stated at the start of this work, I lost a great many times in my life, and I have lost loved ones, but the fight goes on, even through this Long Dark Winter, which I liken to Valley Forge. And I have come to realize that failure is sometimes the first step toward success. "Lay me down and bleed awhile," Reagan said in 1976, when he lost his first bid to become President. "Though I am wounded, I am not slain." As the Great Communicator said, "I shall rise and fight again." He did ... and, God willing, America will as well!

This, my friends, is our time to rise and fight again! It is a defining moment in the history of our nation. Right here, right now, it begins—A time of great responsibility to be greatly borne. Let it be said of us that we mastered our moment, we kept what President Ronald Reagan called our "rendezvous with destiny," and we refused to let America go quietly into the night.

When the first chapter of the history books opening the 21st Century are written, let it be said of us—we happy few, we band of brothers—that we kept faith with our Founding Fathers, we stood in the gap, and, in what would have been the final days of our Republic, we never gave up the fight. We must never give up the fight!

My friends, Pax Americana is at an end. But unlike Rome and Great Britain, this does not necessarily mean the end of

America's era as the preeminent force for good in the world. We have it within our power to break the cycle of history, but we must seize a vision of boldness for America's future. We can reclaim the legal and moral high ground that fueled the Great American Spirit throughout our history, we can defend America's territorial integrity, finish building a great wall to our south, deport those who illegally violated our borders and exist here as criminals, rebuild our military and honor the Veterans who answered their country's call, especially our wounded warriors.

Do these themes sound familiar? They should. They are part of the bold vision of one candidate who became President against the odds, Donald J. Trump. Now we must fight the good fight and continue to defend and champion our Christian values and the Constitution! We truly can make America great again!

This is the challenge of our time … To take a stand for America! This is what it means to be an American, and what we are called to be. And I believe the thoughts and ideas I have articulated in this work were shared by our Founding Fathers and are still shared by the silent majority of Americans today, with implications that reach far beyond the bounds of personal self-interest.

I pray this work will be a wake-up call to the once Silent Majority, a call to action, and a source of hope and encouragement as we take *The Long Way Home.*

In 1775, Paul Revere entered the town of Lexington. It was around midnight, and he had a wake up message for the citizens: "The British are coming! The British are coming!"

The following morning, 700 British soldiers entered the town and were met by 70 citizen-soldiers on the Common. "Here once the embattled farmers stood," Emerson wrote, "and fired the shot heard round the world."

Today, we hear another call. A call to arms. We are at war on many fronts. A new kind of war against anarchists in our streets, Communist China's war against the West, a global Muslim caliphate, and a war to confront an unprecedented attack against our children, our economy, our military, our sovereignty, our cultural heritage, and our legal system. This is a war between the forces of good and evil for the survival of America and the last remnants of civilization. We cannot afford to lose!

If ever there was a time of need, a time for men and women of courage and good will to step forward and be counted, this is such a time. A time for you and I to stand in the gap for America and what remains of Western Civilization and the Rule of Law. We can make this last best hope for man on earth great again! Now that would be a very American thing to do! God willing, our goal will be achieved!

Now is the time to take *The Long Way Home* and return America to her Founding Christian Principles.

As Presidents Reagan and Trump challenged us in the recent past, **Let's Make America Great Again** and fulfill the promise that America's best days are yet to come!

God bless you, and God bless America!

Jesus said unto him,
Thou shalt love the Lord thy God with all thy heart,
and with all thy soul, and with all thy mind.

This is the first and great commandment.
And the second is like unto it,
Thou shalt love thy neighbour as thyself.

On these two commandments hang all the law and the prophets.

~ Matthew 22:37-40

If my people, which are called by my name,
shall humble themselves, and pray, and seek my face,
and turn from their wicked ways;
then will I hear from heaven, and will forgive their sin,
and will heal their land.

~ 2 Chronicles 7:14

## About the Author

# Judge Hal Moroz

Whether therefore ye eat, or drink, or whatsoever ye do,
do all to the glory of God.

~ Psalm 37:23

Judge Hal Moroz was a candidate for Justice on the Supreme Court of Georgia on the June 9th, 2020 Election, which was also the Presidential Primary Election in the Great State of Georgia. Although he lost his race, Judge Moroz garnered nearly half-a-million votes from across the state and brought national attention to the problems facing our modern judiciary.

Hal Moroz is an Attorney and Counselor at Law, who served as an Assistant District Attorney, a County Judge, and a city Chief Judge in the great State of Georgia. His practice in the law has ranged from prosecuting criminals on behalf of the State of Georgia to representing American military veterans in courts up to and including the Supreme Court of the United States.

Judge Moroz is also an accomplished soldier and statesman, as well as a retired U.S. Army officer, having served in the Airborne Infantry. Judge Moroz served on the faculty of Florida Coastal School of Law in Jacksonville, Florida, and the State Bar of Georgia's Institute for Continuing Legal Education (ICLE) in the education of attorneys. He is a former candidate for the U.S. Congress, and served as Special Counsel to the Georgia Republican Party's First Congressional District Committee in the 2000 primary and general elections.

Hal Moroz frequently serves as a news and political commentator, sharing his insight of the law and politics on a variety of popular media programs. He is also a prolific writer, having authored numerous legal articles, weekly legal newspaper columns, and books. Copies of his many books can be ordered at Amazon.com or any major bookstore!

Hal Moroz can be reached through an internet search
or through his email at: hal@morozlaw.com or his website:
MorozLaw.com

I am an American who lives in the shadow of the Cross ...

I walk humbly before God,
I stand tall before men,
And I stand in the gap for America!

~ Judge Hal Moroz

www.ingramcontent.com/pod-product-compliance
Lightning Source LLC
Chambersburg PA
CBHW062142150726
47991CB00006B/2144